Game, Set and Match

Best Wishes

Tony Blair and Father Caden
Church and State, a formidable partnership

Game, Set and Match

John Caden

The Pentland Press Limited
Edinburgh • Cambridge • Durham • USA

First published in 1997 by
The Pentland Press Ltd.
1 Hutton Close
South Church
Bishop Auckland
Durham

British Library Cataloguing in Publication Data.
A Catalogue record for this book is available
from the British Library.

ISBN 1 85821 541 2

Typeset by CBS, Felixstowe, Suffolk
Printed and bound by Antony Rowe Ltd., Chippenham

These memoirs are dedicated to all whose lives I may have touched in nearly a half-century of priesthood, whether in Darlington, Sunderland or Dipton. Especially, I dedicate them to the parishioners, past and present, of St John Fisher, Sedgefield, and to all those who worked alongside me in my forty years' service with the NHS.

CONTENTS

ILLUSTRATIONS

FOREWORD

I was delighted when I heard that Father John Caden had been persuaded to write some memoirs of his very long and interesting priesthood.

Father John's years as a priest have covered almost half a century since his ordination in 1948. They have spanned two completely contrasting eras. He was well acquainted with and worked at the grass roots in the very traditional pre-Vatican II world, but readily adapted himself to the demanding changes of the post-1965 Church.

In his earlier priesthood, apart from his usual pastoral duties he was a pioneer in the Church's Apostolate of Youth. He also had a very unusual and fascinating Apostolate of the Theatre during the eight years of his work in Sunderland as Catholic Stage Guild Chaplain.

When he was appointed to St John Fisher, Sedgefield in 1966 he worked tirelessly in improving the quality of life of all those who lived in Sedgefield and County Durham, and not just those who were members of his own flock. His perception of the Mission of the Church was that of a church that helped build Community. To this end he became known far and wide as someone who would help everybody. He worked as a Town Councillor and for nearly twenty years as a Durham County Councillor. During those years, as well as working as Chaplain to the Sedgefield Hospitals he also used his NHS patient-experience in selfless voluntary work in the administration and management of the NHS. Amidst other work he was Chairman of Sunderland Community Health Council and Vice-Chairman of South-West Durham Health Authority for sixteen years in all.

It was in 1983 that our paths crossed for the first time, when Tony and I became regular worshippers at his Sedgefield Church. In due course he baptised our children in St John Fisher, and became a dear friend as well as our spiritual guide and parish priest. His priesthood has all the vibrancy that stems naturally from its foundation on his gospel values . . . gospel values which have become a very natural part of his whole persona.

I think you will find these memoirs heart-warming and interesting. They will give you some insights, often poignant and not without humour, into the life and training of a real priest, not just a 'character' conjured up by the media!

Cherie Blair

PREFACE

In August 1995, I was invited to Marlow by Fiona Doonican, entertainer Val Doonican's daughter. She had asked me to marry her in the picturesque Catholic church by the side of the River Thames. Fiona was marrying Julian Parker, a young builder from the area. The wedding, incidentally, proved to be quite memorable: a nuptial mass in a wonderful setting. St Peter's Church was only about fifty yards from the River Thames landing stage opposite The Compleat Angler. This famous hotel was the venue for the reception. Julian and Fiona went there, not by limousine but in a gaily-festooned river barge. After the reception they asked me if I would be willing to baptize their first child, if and when their first child was born. A year later, Bethany Louise arrived! I explained that if their new parish priest was willing, I would come down and perform the ceremony. We completed the pre-baptism talk over dinner the night before. The following day we celebrated the baptism during a special mass. Bethany Louise was the first Bethany I had ever baptized in hundreds of baptisms.

I stayed with Val and Lynn his wife for a couple of nights. Val and I had been close friends since 1953. As a young performer with a group called The Four Ramblers he had come to Sunderland Empire. Lynnette Ray, his wife, was a well-known singer and pantomime principal boy of the 1950s, and had approached me in 1961 to receive instruction in the Catholic Faith before she was to marry Val. Throughout our forty-three years of friendship, Val and I have never missed a year without 'getting together'. Our conversations on these occasions were always spontaneous and wide-ranging. They could cover anything from the laughter-filled episodes of his star-studded show business career, to the recent developments in the Catholic Church and on the theological scene. I knew many of the stories Val could tell of his fifty years in the business. Likewise, Val had heard many of the interesting stories of my fifty years in the parochial priesthood! On that evening after his granddaughter's baptism we were talking late into the night. He reminded me that he had already put down on paper some of the poignant memories and events of his fifty years, when he wrote his autobiographical books *Walking Tall* and *The Special Years.* These memoirs were not to be lost to posterity.

However, to my surprise, he insisted that many of my memoirs could be valuable. They portrayed a picture of the secular priesthood that was never really known, even to people within the Church, let alone to people outside it! He continued, 'The Catholic priests of *Bless me Father* and *Father Ted* were so often just a caricature of what priesthood was really about. Some reflections of real priesthood, the kind of reflections I had often shared with him, would be a revelation to many. Young people today need to know why their churches are still available to them. They should know what priesthood has really been about for half a century.' I agreed that in the 1990s publicity about priesthood was frequently, at best, negative, but at worst, positively harmful! He asked me had I ever kept a diary. I told him that I had always worked in parishes where I seemed to be working a twelve-hour day! I had never had the time to jot things down. He summed up, 'Father, if you don't jot them down your stories will never be told, they will die with you!'

So after more exchanges, he made me promise to find an extra hour in my busy daily schedule to put something on paper or on tape.

The following pages, I hope, will give some little insight into what priesthood was about in the 1940s, when there was a comparative glut of vocations to the Catholic priesthood. They may cast some light on how a typical grass-roots priesthood was lived out for almost half a century. They may even provide food for thought as to what priesthood should be about as we approach the Millenium.

ACKNOWLEDGEMENTS

These memoirs could never have seen the light of day without the patient and dedicated work of my secretary friends, Eleanor Maddison and Colette Wood. My sincere thanks also to Father Leo Coughlin presently spreading the gospel message in Las Vegas.

My thanks, too, to my nephew, Martin Parker and friend Barry Jackson for their photographic input. I am grateful also to friends who gave me valuable advice during the compilation of the memoirs.

CHAPTER I

A NEW PRIME MINISTER

'TON-Y, TON-Y, Tonee, Tonee,' the crowds chanted . . . as the Right Honourable Anthony Linton Blair, the new Prime Minister, got out of the limousine that had whisked him away from his historic meeting with the Queen. Instead of the Downing Street gates being opened to admit the Prime Minister's car, the car stopped in Whitehall! Tony and Cherie began the final sixty yards of their journey to Number Ten on foot, something quite unprecedented in Downing Street takeovers!

As they reached out to scores of rapturously cheering, waving fans and helpers, who vied with each other for a handshake, a touch or a smile of recognition, the security officers went through acrobatic agonies as they tried to do their job! Even though the hundreds of people crowding the Downing Street pavements had all been carefully vetted as friends or media personnel, there was always the slight chance that somebody might have obtained a press permit unlawfully. No wonder the security men looked anxious on this the first real test of their abilities with the new Prime Minister! However, all went well. It took Tony and Cherie a good fifteen minutes to reach the space in front of Number Ten. Some final adjustments were made to the positioning of the microphones, and then the new Prime Minister addressed the nation and the world. In his first official speech as Prime Minister he made a pledge to the nation: 'This is not a mandate for dogma or for doctrine but a mandate to get those things done in our country that desperately need doing for the future . . . and this new Labour Government will govern in the interests of all our people – the whole of this nation, that I can promise you!'

At the end of his speech tumultuous applause echoed round Downing Street. The Blair children and Cherie materialized from the

Outside 10 Downing Street after Election victory

edge of the crowd near the doorway of Number Ten, and the family lined up for the photocalls as the world's media focused on them. I was standing near the door of Number Ten with a group of children and their mothers. They were from the Blairs' London church of St Joan of Arc in Islington. As I gulped hard to hold back the emotion and tears of joy, I carefully watched the children and their reactions. These were the children whom I had baptized nearly three hundred miles away in Sedgefield! I noticed Euan and his brother Nicholas were quite dazed by the magnitude of the moment. Only little Kathryn seemed to be actually enjoying it! As the family finally moved back inside, and the door of Number Ten closed behind them, I prayed a silent but fervent prayer that they would be given the resilience and grace to cope with the tremendous pressures that must now be part of their everyday living. I knew as that door closed, that a new ere had begun - life for us in Sedgefield and Trimdon would never be quite the same again. We would never be able to enjoy again that casual intimacy that we had enjoyed in the constituency for fourteen years. I thought wistfully of a July day last year when I had dropped into the family home in Trimdon. Tony was busy on the phone when I arrived. Euan 'commandeered' me with the innocent invitation : 'Father Caden, did you ever play cricket?' 'Yes,' I replied! I was eagerly steered out of the back door and into the garden to take the place of their father who had been called to the phone. I can remember Euan's look of amazement when I was able to recall with some confidence the lessons I had learned fifty-five years before on 'How to play a straight bat'. After that, I vied with Nicholas for who would bowl me out first. Eventually, Tony rejoined us, and we had a wonderful, family half-hour with two-a-side and everybody fielding! Of course our Sedgefield friend had overnight suddenly moved from the national stage to emerge as a potential 'collossus' on the world stage - it would never be quite the same again. I couldn't help but think of John the Baptist in the gospel story - inevitably John's prominent role in preparing the centre stage for Jesus, the Messiah, had of its very nature to become a supporting one. Nevertheless, it was a vitally important role at the time.

I will write much more in due course about Tony Blair's interaction with the community, families and friends here in his Sedgefield constituency, and will recall how a tennis-strengthened friendship which began in 1983 finally became Game, Set and Match at Number Ten Downing Street on 2 May 1997!

CHAPTER II

CHILDHOOD - EARLY YEARS

I suspect it must have been when my mother was about to give birth to my sister Mary - most births were still at home, of course, in the 1920s. I was 'farmed out' for a few days to my grandmother, who lived in Whitburn Street, West Hartlepool. Yes, West Hartlepool and Hartlepool were two separate boroughs in those days.

I was about twenty months old at the time and I was late in learning to walk. I could scramble, crawl and almost walk a bit. My grandmother, a pious woman who regularly attended St Joseph's Church, took me out in the pram and decided to call into St Joseph's to pay 'a visit' to the Lord, as it was termed. She took the pram into the porch, took me out of it and carried me down to the front pews. With her eyes on the altar and the tabernacle, she failed to notice that I had made my escape. Later, she told my mother that 'the little fella' had scuttled off, and was heading towards the steps of the large and ornate pulpit. My grandmother was a large woman, and certainly was very slow on her feet; by the time she had almost caught up with me, I had already crawled onto the second step of the pulpit. Apparently, realizing that capture was now inevitable, I suddenly looked round from my vantage point and in a loud voice exclaimed 'God'!

My mother would insist, when she told the story, that I was looking towards the altar - I had been taken to church several times already, so maybe I did have some sense of direction; on the other hand, we did have at home a prominent picture of *The Finding of the Child Jesus in the Temple.*

My mother, though a wonderful Catholic, was prone to a little superstition. She liked to read the tea leaves in the cups. Even in later life she resisted the temptation to use teabags. She preferred loose Typhoo tea because she could see the tea leaves at the end of a cup of tea. She was also not averse to the odd interpretation of a dream, and she *frequently* had dreams. No wonder my mother wondered whether the escape in St Joseph's Church in March 1925 and my first word from the pulpit could have a greater significance! Time alone would tell.

However, I suppose it all really started when I was an altar boy in St Cuthbert's in West Hartlepool. St Cuthbert's was a parish which had been cut off from the mother-parish of St Joseph's. The church was for many years just a church hall that had a dual use. Nevertheless, there was quite a phalanx of altar boys. When I was about nine years of age I was trained rather rigorously by Joe and Billy Devine, twin brothers and senior altar boys. The Mass, of course, was the Latin Mass, the Tridentine Mass. We were drilled in learning the Latin responses, and were conditioned 'in wiping the smile from our faces'. Gradually, and eventually, we would aspire to take the thurible at Benediction. Ultimately, we rose to the dizzy heights of being entrusted with the Cross as cross-bearer. The parish priest was Father O'Sullivan, known to his parishioners as 'John Paul' or 'Father O'. He was a talented man, a scholar and a musician who also liked to drive a fast car! I can remember as far back as 1933 being taken to a schoolboys' camp with other altar boys in his Jowett-Javelin, and actually seeing the needle flicker to eighty miles per hour! He never knew that there would be two Popes called John Paul before the close of the century. The first would only grace the papacy for a month, the second would be the first non-Italian Pope for centuries, a Pope who would come from behind the Iron Curtain, a Pope who many would say would be indirectly instrumental in the crumbling of that same Iron Curtain. His inspiration for Solidarity, the first trade union movement since the emergence of Russia as a world power, is well documented.

There were two curates – Father Hugh Dowd and Father Tony Cunningham. Father Dowd was the senior curate. He was a smiling, courteous man, dark and of medium height. He used to wear a trilby hat and one of my memories is of him frequently raising it. He quickly became a role model for me. His memory is deeply etched despite the very few years I had contact with him. In 1939 he would leave the parish scene to serve in the War as an army chaplain. He would spend the remainder of his life in the Army, rising to become Senior Chaplain to the Forces. Father Tony Cunningham would leave St Cuthbert's, West Hartlepool and would spend many of his priestly years in teaching and as a hard-working parish priest in Bishop Auckland. Our future paths as priests and educationalists would frequently cross. Father Tony was a charming, cultured man who had great zest for life, and scorned 'retirement'. He would eventually die in harness and suffered a heart attack while taking Holy Communion to the sick. True to form, he was looking forward at the time to his golden jubilee as a priest. He was actually awaiting delivery of a new computer-cum-word processor.

And now, a little anecdote about Father Hugh Dowd. As a very young curate in West Hartlepool, he was visiting my Aunt Mabel. My grandfather, Reuben Palmer, who had lived all his eighty-two years as a very staunch Irish Protestant, had come to spend his last few years with his daughter, Mabel. During one of Father Dowd's visits to Aunt Mabel, grandfather Reuben had idly wondered aloud 'whether it was too late to become a papist'. In 1930, of course, papist was a term of some opprobrium for a Catholic.

Understandably, Father Hugh decided not to pursue things further until his next visit. A few days afterwards, he related the incident to his Irish parish priest, Father O'Sullivan. 'Father O' told him to go back immediately and talk to Reuben. Sadly, it was too late - Reuben had died quietly during the night. It was to be my first introduction to something the theologians would call 'baptism of desire'. Father Dowd may have slipped up with Reuben; however, I am sure that he can now square that in Heaven with the knowledge that he was undoubtedly the role model for priesthood for the writer of these present lines!

My short career as an altar boy at St Cuthbert's awakened in me a boyish desire 'to become a priest like Father Dowd'. Don't think that I was in any way pious or different from other boys. Playing football was my greatest passion, in fact, was almost an obsession. When I made my first Communion, fasting from midnight the night before was the norm, to be eligible to receive Holy Communion on the following day. At that time my regular Saturday morning routine at the age of ten was to go and serve Mass at 9 a.m.; I would take my football boots with me, as indeed would another altar boy friend of

As a boy - playing cricket

mine, Owen Murray. Owen was later to become a Mill Hill missionary priest and serve in Pakistan for almost thirty years. After Mass, we would hurry straight from church to the Rift House recreation ground where we would meet a friend, Gerry Roberton. The chance to play with real goalposts, rather than just putting down our coats for goals, was an opportunity for our imaginations to run riot. Suddenly, we were gracing the Victoria Ground which was the home of Hartlepool United. Suddenly, we became the very people we read about in the *Football Mail.* I would go home to Tristram Avenue for my breakfast about 11.30 a.m. I can now well understand why my mother would scold me with 'Football will be the death of you'. She knew that supper on Friday night was the last time I had eaten or drunk anything. Yes, I was very much a normal boy!

Eventually, I told my parents that I wanted to become a priest like Father Dowd. I look back now and think that this was a bigger shock to my father than to my mother. My father worked very hard, and very often unsocial hours, for the London & North Eastern Railway. I think he had a secret wish that his son would never have to go out to work at 6 a.m. or midnight, and cycle two or three miles to start work on a railway. He used to talk to me about 'sticking in' with my studies and passing a Civil Service exam, or becoming a customs officer. The thought of my becoming a priest, I don't think had even crossed his mind. However, he agreed to my mother talking to Father O'Sullivan who, to put it mildly, wasn't very encouraging. Father O'Sullivan was obviously anxious to assure himself that the vocation was mine and not my mother's. Despite his attitude, he did finally arrange for me to have a screening interview with the Seminary Screening Board, and eventually, after being accepted, I started my studies at Ushaw College in September 1935 at the age of twelve.

CHAPTER III

THE SEMINARY, 1935-48

In my later years I was constantly explaining to people who were not Catholics, or even to the younger generation of Catholics, what junior seminary training was all about! The junior seminary was for the education and training of boys from the age of eleven, who would then continue to study for School Certificate and Higher School Certificate - the equivalent of our present GCSEs and A levels. They would continue their education and training on the same campus. It was about testing and training, as well as about education. It was about testing your boyhood aspirations to priesthood, and seeing if there was really a vocation to priesthood lying beneath them. During the 1930s and 1940s it was common practice to interview and segregate boys from the age of eleven. They would leave home and continue their studies at a boarding school, in this case, the seminary. Here they would be cut off completely from family and from the outside world. The regime was positively spartan, as indeed, of course, were the regimes of many of our expensive public schools at the time, like Ampleforth and Downside. The rules were very strict, the food was very plain and never too much of it. There was plenty of sport and plenty of prayer. In retrospect, it was only the companionship of the other students and the plentiful opportunities for sport that made life bearable. Indeed, for many of us, it made it quite enjoyable. I have said already that the regime was intended to separate us from the outside world. This intention was made readily possible by the physical location of the college, for it was on the top of a hill about four miles outside of Durham. There were no houses or dwellings within half a mile of Ushaw. The city of Durham, its shops and buses, were all out of bounds. We were not allowed newspapers or radios, and so we were effectively unaware of what was happening in the world outside.

Occasionally one of the students would have cuttings from a sports paper sent to him from home, and there might be some news of the outside world on the back of the sports page, but by and large our mail was censored and checked.

In our very early years, discipline and the keeping of the rules were very, very important. The breaking of sometimes rather trivial rules could result in rather severe 'corporal punishment'. Discipline and keeping of the rules were very carefully watched. The inability to comply with them at a high level would frequently result in students being expelled. However, alongside the discipline, study was equally important. Our studies concentrated very much on the Classics: Latin, Greek, French, English and History were taken for granted, and we had to take them at the equivalent of GCSE. Later, in the equivalent of A levels, there was very little choice. Latin and Greek were the main subjects, along with either French or English. Roman History was also a popular subject. In the 1940s, Ushaw had resisted siren calls to become an adjunct or part of Durham University. In those days, the academic standards at Ushaw were very high, especially in Classics: Latin, Greek, Roman History, Greek History; these were 'bread-and-butter' subjects. Of course, we had no distractions and had every opportunity for concentration. Teenage boys at Ushaw rarely, if ever, saw a girl during their college years, let alone enjoyed their company! It may have been partly for this reason that formal links with Durham University were resisted. Such links might not have readily predisposed a student for a life of celibacy.

CHAPTER IV

THE SYSTEM

The Ushaw education was entirely geared to equipping the student to be a man of culture and letters - someone who would have a broad, all-round education, enabling him to be articulate, a clear thinker and logical. His A level equivalents were taken with the Oxford and Cambridge Joint Board. This particular board had the highest standard in Classics in the whole country. Latin and Greek were the core subjects, with another A level in either English or French. Durham University could have benefitted from a Classics link with the Ushaw of 1940! Indeed, I remember doing Durham University BA papers as a practise for our Oxford & Cambridge Joint Board exam. In fact, the link would not happen for another quarter of a century.

A sound education to us was just a preparation for pastoral, secular priesthood. After A levels we would proceed immediately, again on the same campus, to a course of two years in Philosophy, Physiology, Logic and Church History. This would then be followed by a further four years of Theology and Sacred Scripture. After that, ordination and reporting for parish work as young priests in our own dioceses. Most of us dreaded any mention of a degree course being interposed between A levels and the final six years of Philosophy and Theology. If it was proposed, then we would have to go to Cambridge with the sure knowledge that we would eventually be drafted back to teach in the very seminary where we had already spent thirteen years!

I have said already that study, along with discipline, was all important. If a certain standard was not achieved then you were politely asked to leave. However, another part of the regime was 'compulsory' exercise. We had our own swimming baths in the college, which, in the 1940s, were rather basic, but later on, in the 1960s, they became a very desirable bonus; indeed, I can remember in the 1960s, as a priest

I always chose Ushaw for my annual retreat because I could enjoy some exercise in the swimming baths while trying to recharge my spiritual batteries. During my thirteen years as a student at the seminary, I played football three or four times a week. Cricket was also available and later in the college course, tennis and golf. The college had its own nine-hole golf course which was available to the divinity students - those who were in the last four years of the seminary course. With thousands of opportunities to practise, I developed a competence in most sports available, but especially in football and cricket.

Football had been my natural sport since boyhood. Encouragement and coaching came from young teachers who were delayed two or three years in their priestly training course in order to act as teachers in secular subjects or as games masters. This meant that their complete seminary course might last sixteen years before they were finally allocated to parishes in their own diocese. A youngster would sign on for a diocese at the start of his course, and later, would continue to work for that diocese after ordination until his old age.

I remember, in particular, one of these 'minor professors' as they were called, who had a profound effect on my college days. Gerard McLean helped me in what seemed at the time to be an endless course. 'Gerry' as he was known, was later to become Bishop of Middlesbrough - one of the few bishops in my earlier years who did not have a Roman Graduate or Post Graduate background! Gerry was a brilliant all-round sportsman. He excelled in football, cricket, golf and tennis. He became a serious role model for me in my seminary days, just as Father Dowd had influenced my childhood. Many were the times he would smile and shake his head in disbelief when, as an eighteen-year-old goalkeeper, I managed to save one of his rasping drives! That smile did more for my self-esteem than all the medals and trophies I would later win in competitions in Teeside, Darlington, Sunderland and Dipton. I was 'signed up' for the Hexham and Newcastle diocese, and 'Gerry' became the Bishop of Middlesbrough, our neighbouring diocese, so he was never my own bishop. However, as a young parish priest in Sedgefield in 1968, I would go over to the Bishop McLean Charity Ball at the Marton Country Club, and have a joke about our Ushaw years. I reminded him that once as a fifteen-year-old in 1940, I was playing my 'master' in the final of a billiards tournament. The balls really ran for me that day, and I can remember Bishop McLean's wry remark to me was, 'John, I hope you will remember, that proficiency at billiards is a sign of a misspent youth.'

I cracked back, rather irreverently, 'You must have misspent yours, sir!'

Back in 1940 billiards had not yet been overtaken by snooker as the popular sport. It was the age of television around the 1980s when snooker became the popular TV drama that it still is today.

I have referred to the spartan regime of my thirteen years training in the seminary. It was geared to produce single-minded young men who were conditioned to a life of obedience and dedication. Men who would accept 'postings' or 'appointments' from their bishop without query or comment. In the interests of 'spreading the Gospel message' they would follow the bishop's commands or those of the parish priest to whom the bishop had appointed them, as indicative of the will of God. Such blind obedience, I realize, must now seem completely unbelievable. Indeed, it was the Vatican Council of 1959-63 to which I will later refer, that was responsible for changing 'blind' obedience into 'reasoned' obedience.

In this moulding of single-minded young men, one of the dimensions that was taken for granted, and was never even queried in my training years, was celibacy. From our earliest years, it was made clear to us that if we wanted to bring the Gospel message to the world, we could only finally do this as celibate priests. If we wanted to be ordained as priests, we had to accept it as a necessary precondition - a man had to give up the idea of a wife and children. Indeed, the very 'thought' of having a deep friendship with a woman was unacceptable. As the priest-writer Lacordaire wrote of priesthood, 'The priest had to be a member of all families, yet belonging to none.' We students thought that this was something that could be achieved if we dedicated our lives and our ministry one hundred per cent to spreading the message of the Gospel. Somehow, God would help us to overcome the challenge, even though it might appear to be against all human odds!

Our seminary training ensured that we would never come into contact with women, except a few women of 'advanced years' who worked in the college in cleaning and cooking. There were no 'open days' at Ushaw between 1936 and 1948 when families might have been welcomed, and no visitors from the outside world were ever welcomed during my thirteen years at Ushaw. You saw your family only twice a year, during the Christmas and summer vacations. Parents, brothers and sisters were forbidden to visit. Many boys found the homesickness and isolation too much. The drop-out rate from an initial class of thirty-five could easily be 80 per cent at the end of the thirteen years.

THE WEXFORD INVASION

You can well imagine our amazement when in 1943 there was a sudden invasion of Irish colleens. A small group of Irish nuns had arrived at the college to supervise domestic chores - cooking, cleaning etc. To help them achieve this, they imported about a dozen fifteen- and sixteen-year-old girls from their native Wexford. One of the girls was allocated to each corridor or area of the college. I lived at the time on a corridor ironically known as 'Paradise'. Our allocation was a real live girl whom we residents of Paradise nicknamed Wendy. I say 'nicknamed' advisedly because we were not allowed to talk to any of the maids or have any conversation with them whatsoever. Such familiarity would have led to our instant expulsion. Even though all conversation was forbidden, the girls were sometimes anxious to please. They would remove personal belongings from the students' rooms, like football socks or handkerchiefs for washing and darning. Wendy was no exception: on a couple of occasions she removed my mud-stained football stockings or performed some other act of kindness for one of my fellow students. There would be a knock at the door during our private study period when we were supposed to stay in our rooms and work. The awful worry at the time was that the 'prefect of studies' might be patrolling the area outside our doors at the same time as some dark beauty would emerge from a student's room. Wendy would receive at best a brief and embarrassed 'thank you', followed by a fervent prayer that she would not have been seen emerging from the room.

The original Wexford invasion did not last very long. Most of the original contingent soon found that they could earn much more money by working in a munitions factory, or on a sugar-beet farm in Lincolnshire. Wendy disappeared along with several others. Later I heard that she had gone to Lincolnshire when she departed from Paradise corridor. She sent a postcard to me from Lincoln saying that she was happy there with a crowd of Irish workers, although I never actually received it for it was intercepted by the censorship system of the time. Then there was some high-level discussion as to whether I should be ordained at all! It was eventually decided that my ordination to what was a major step to the priesthood at the time - the sub-diaconate - would be postponed, even though I had assured the authorities at the college that I had never had any correspondence with Wendy, let alone any friendship. She had merely sent an open postcard to me on impulse. However, even though my superiors were harbouring doubts about my priestly potential at the time, my own peers had no such doubts. They elected me to the only formal post of liaison between the ninety-strong divinity student body and the college authorities - a post which I held until I was ordained in 1948.

After my ordination, I was appointed as a priest in Darlington. Out of the blue, I received a letter from Wendy congratulating me on my ordination. She had evidently heard about the ordination from some Wexford friend who had remained at the college. By that time she was married and living in Upper New York State. I sent her my ordination card, a spiritual souvenir card which it was customary for newly ordained priests to give to their friends. She later sent me photographs of her husband, Bud, and her children, but inevitably, with the pressure of my life and work, we lost contact. It was going to be forty-five years later that I would receive a telephone call from Ireland in 1995. Wendy's husband had died and she was visiting her family in Ireland. She had discovered my telephone number in Sedgefield from the Sunderland church where I had worked in 1951. We had a long phone conversation, but sadly we could not meet up as she was due to return to the States a couple of days later. She was genuinely shocked that her innocent postcard of 1941 had very nearly finished my career as a priest before it had even started! Since then we have exchanged greetings at Christmas. Perhaps one day, Wendy, we will meet up again when you visit Ireland. We will have such a lot of news to exchange.

CHAPTER V

SEMINARY DAYS IN RETROSPECT - VATICAN II

When I look back from 1996 over half a century to my Ushaw days, which stretched from 1936 to 1948, I often wonder how I ever lasted the course. When I talk about those training days to young priests of today, it is clear that they think I am just 'telling stories' to amuse or to shock.

The truth is that the Vatican Council of 1962-5 changed the life of the Church and its members so radically that few people who were born after 1960 can even begin to imagine what life was really like before Pope John XXIII. In January 1959 Pope John XXIII summoned the Vatican Council, which was an international congress of bishops, archbishops and cardinals from all over the world, held in Rome. He called together about 3,500 bishops to discuss matters that were vital to the teaching, customs and disciplines of the Church. The Council itself would last three years. The previous international congress of this nature had been held one hundred years before. Those were the days of stagecoaches and sailing ships, and even though every bishop in the world was entitled to attend, in practice, only a small proportion would ever get there. However, in 1959 we were already in the age of very speedy transportation. The liner *Queen Elizabeth* was criss-crossing the Atlantic; jet airliners like the Boeing 707 were already linking all parts of the world at 500 miles per hour. The Vatican Council that John XXIII would summon would bring together every bishop in the Catholic world, not just those who could travel overland to Rome in Europe. I can remember as a young priest in Sunderland in 1959 feeling a surge of excitement, along with my fellow priests, when the new Pope announced that he was summoning a new Vatican Council.

JOHN XXIII - VATICAN II

Pope John XXIII was a very interesting choice as Pope. We had seen a long papacy, ending in 1958 with the death of Pope Pius XII. Pius XII was a very 'private' Pope. In those days, if Catholics wanted to see the Pope, they had to visit Rome. Pius XII rarely left the Vatican, except to go to a holiday villa a few miles away at Castelgandolfo for a short summer holiday. I suspect that some of the cardinals whose job it was to choose a new Pope when they met in what is known as a Conclave felt that a future Pope should be prepared to use the modern methods of travel. He should go and see the people, rather than just wait for the 'people of the world' to come and see him during a pilgrimage to Rome. After a long period of conservative papacy some cardinals were ready for a change. One of the front-runner candidates for such change was a young Cardinal called Montini, who was Archbishop of Milan. However, Montini was a mere sixty-one years of age: if elected, he could be Pope for a very long time. Obviously, most of the cardinals decided that caution should be exercised on this occasion. There would be plenty of time in the future for Cardinal Montini, if they now elected a candidate who was prudent, and yet elderly. Cardinal Roncalli, at seventy-eight, was ideally such a candidate. When he became Pope he took the name of John XXIII. Few could have imagined the world-shattering repercussions of this election. Here was a man who had spent much of his priesthood in ambassadorial roles in countries where the Catholic Church was often a minority interest. He fully understood that even though as Pope he governed some 800 million Catholics in the world, billions of people lived in a world that did not readily understand Catholicism and many of its customs and practices. Suffice to say that he amazed thousands of his priests and millions of his people. He decided that, far from just concentrating on his prayer life in the Vatican, he was going to throw open its windows; he was going to let in the fresh air of change to blow through it. John XXIII called it an '*aggiorniamento*'! He announced to the world in January 1959 that he was calling another Vatican Council - it would be known as Vatican II - and he set in place the machinery for its organisation.

This Vatican Council would look at the Catholic Church as it was at that time. It would also look at many of its practices and their implications for a multi-cultural and multi-religious world. Those long years spent by Pope John XXIII in his pre-papacy days had given him some very special insights.

He knew how billions of people outside the Catholic Church perceived us as Catholics. He was determined to make sure that whatever the Catholic Church would decide about its future in the second half of the twentieth century, there would be ample consultation with other Christian and non-Christian bodies from the very outset. Now this in hindsight does not appear to be very momentous, and yet, to someone like myself, who in the first ten years of his priesthood had never formally worshipped in a non-Catholic church, or never formally welcomed non-Catholics to our own church services, it was indeed momentous. No wonder that the second Vatican Council became known as the 'Ecumenical Council'. With John XXIII, ecumenism or unity among Christians, had become the bottom line of the Gospel message!

In addition to inviting the 3,500 bishops from every corner of the earth, Pope John formally invited 70 or 80 observers from other Christian churches. These were not merely to be bodily present at all the sessions of the Vatican Council: they were to be consulted about the content of the agenda, and more importantly, at the way the agenda would be presented. This would ensure that their views and sensitivities about the Gospel message of Christ were reflected at every formal session of the Council. They would not take any active part in the debates, but they would not need to do so - their views would already be reflected in the eventual wording of the agenda. There would also be consultation before the final press conferences took place. This meant that our fellow-Christian leaders, who were observers at Vatican II, had probably much more involvement in the shaping of the final decrees of the Council, than thousands of ordinary priests who were working at the grass roots throughout the Catholic world. I state this without any sense of grievance or rancour! Indeed, most of my fellow priests would agree that they endorsed this situation. Some of the outstanding issues of Vatican II, like the gradual change from the old Latin Mass to Mass in the vernacular would be enhanced and made more meaningful by liturgical consultation with fellow Christians from the outset. The vernacular might be French or German or Spanish, as well as English. Obviously, once the Mass was going to be in English, for example, it was important that the millions of English-speaking Catholics should be comfortable with it! Prior to the Council, Catholics throughout the world had worshipped in churches where the priest-celebrant had his 'back' to the congregation most of the time. Because the priest was speaking entirely in Latin, there was no real dialogue. Very few Catholics understood Latin; however, once the Mass was in English, then there had to be real dialogue. Suddenly, the priest had to face his congregation all of the time and the congregation knew exactly what he was saying. He then had to concentrate on the way he delivered his message and managed 'his' part in the dialogue. He had to make eye-to-eye contact with the people in the congregation, and had to sustain this rapport or contact for the forty-five minutes or so of the average Sunday Mass. Many priests of my generation found this a big ordeal: most of them had spent twenty years or more reciting Latin prayers with their backs to the people - prayers which at that time were regarded as associated with the personal sanctification of the priest, rather than with the 'sanctification of the people'. Quite often the people prayed in their own way, often using rosary beads or simple prayer books. A very small percentage used a missal with Latin or English words, rather like using a libretto at an opera.

After the Vatican Council, it was comparatively easy for theologians and liturgists from the Catholic Church, the Anglican Church and other churches to work together on texts for the new English Catholic Mass. They could achieve a certain amount of conformity in the text of the English Mass and the Anglican Prayers and Communion Service. There were many other smaller changes resulting from the Council. I will mention only two of them: Cremation, and the 'Westminster Theatre law'. A revision of these two points was long overdue. Prior to 1959 a Catholic was not allowed to be cremated. Prior to 1959, a Catholic priest was not allowed to attend a live 'theatrical performance' even if that performance was a grand opera or a Shakespearean play. He was allowed to attend the 'cinema', because the wording of the original ban only covered 'live theatrical performances', and therefore did not cover the cinema which was not a 'live performance'. Just how completely out of date this law was, I was to find out between 1951 and 1961, when one of my pastoral jobs would be to act as Chaplain to the Catholic Stage Guild - I will dwell further on this part of my priestly life later in these memoirs!

I could continue to write at great length about the Vatican Council. I would not want to risk boring would-be readers; therefore, reluctantly, I will not now go into any more details here. Suffice for me to say, it was, in retrospect, the single most important event of my nearly fifty years of priesthood. If you are to have any inkling of what Catholicism is all about as we approach the Millenium, then it is imperative that you know something of what the second Vatican Council was all about.

I already stressed the importance of the intervention of John XXIII's Council and the impact it had on my developing priesthood. I have been able to retain a zest for my priesthood well into old age. I would be the first to admit that this is largely due to the fact that a most 'Unlikely Pope' gave me a new vision of priesthood. I say 'unlikely Pope' - Pope John XXIII was an unlikely Pope, make no mistake! He always reminded me of a famous boxing promoter of the 1950s - Jack Solomons. During my student days and later years I was always interested in the professional boxing scene: promoter Jack Solomons, complete with his trade mark - the ever-present cigar - was one of the foremost boxing promoters of the time. Somehow, when I looked at photos of Pope John XXIII, I could almost see the tell-tale cigar. He certainly could hold his own when it came to making a lasting deal.

CHAPTER VI

ORDINATION AND THE EARLY YEARS OF PRIESTHOOD

I have touched on the thirteen years of preparation, which I have treated as a continuum, or as a whole. These years demanded a dedicated leaving of home, of family, of loved ones which began for me in 1935. For me, the preparation did not finish until 25 July 1948. Preparation for most professional careers of that time would have been shaped very differently; usually divided into three different components - grammar school days, university years and finally, the launching into one's eventual profession. For me, and scores of others, it was quite different. The beginning, middle and end were to be enacted and completed on the very same campus. This gave it all a sameness and an inevitability which was to prove to be an impossible obstacle to five out of six of those who aspired to achieve it.

However, the big day was drawing nearer. Somehow, I could hardly imagine that it was really happening. The last year or so, especially, was to me somehow almost unreal. I had to pinch myself occasionally to assure myself that I had actually made it all through that never-ending course, yet I had finally arrived at the last lap, despite the handicaps of the earlier part of the race.

Over the years my class of thirty-five had lost most of its earlier members. We had, however, picked up other members along the way. These were boys who had done their School Certificate and Higher School Certificate at other schools and colleges while they had continued to live at home. They represented a different system, but we all fitted in together in a very homogenous way. All of these students would be 'signed up' to work in other dioceses throughout the country, but especially in parts of Lancashire and Yorkshire. Their bishops might have picked different dates for ordaining them, and so we began to say our goodbyes to each other as early as April in that year of 1948. I can well remember the relaxed joy as we helped each other in our 'amateurish' way to prepare for parish life. We would prepare with sermon clubs and 'rehearsals' for 'saying mass'. In these sermon clubs, we would deliver practise sermons to a group of five or six of our fellow student-priests, and would offer criticism to each other. Twenty years later, a Special Professor of Communications would use film and tapes, and later, 'video', to help 'round off' the preaching process for the students of that time.

Without doubt, there was much that was faulty in the system. The thirteen years of seminary training undoubtedly 'conditioned' a student for what would follow later. To use one of my sporting comparisons - the daily grind of miles of 'roadwork' could ensure that the boxer's legs didn't let him down when he needed that extra stamina later in the fight. All his skill would finally be of no avail if his legs 'went' at the crucial stages. However, maybe something more than mere conditioning was needed. Certainly, when I look back, it was the friendship and support of our fellow strivers that indelibly marked our progress to the day of ordination. It helped to make up for the deficiencies of the system, although maybe some of my fellow ordinands didn't see it that way. I had often intended to ask them, but sadly, when the 'goodbyes' came during those last four months between April and July, some of them were to prove final goodbyes. Inevitably, distances and the demands of work were to prove too much of a handicap. Many classes would try to keep in touch by class reunions or 'school dinners', as they were called in Ushaw jargon. I'm afraid the Class of '48 didn't prove to be world beaters in this field! Nevertheless, there *were* classes who proved they could achieve it - the Class of '47, I remember, was one such class! For fifty years they have continued to keep in touch at least annually, despite the loss of many of their members down the years through death. Indeed, through their continued friendship, they eventually reunited one of their fellow students who left them before ordination. He had married and become a director in a well-known 'Gin' company. His children had already grown up, so after the death of his wife, he was easily recruited again, this time by two of his friends in my own diocese of Hexham and

Newcastle. Father Bert Nicholson is still a hard-working parish priest in Billingham and from time to time enjoys the pleasure of being with his own grandchildren.

ORDINATION - FIRST MASS

And so, eventually, 25 July 1948 arrived. We were the last group from the Class of '48 to be ordained: six of us, plus one from an earlier year, who had spent three years teaching at Ushaw before he was finally ordained. It was customary at that time to ordain the students for the Newcastle diocese together as a group at the College. I'm sure some of us would have preferred to be ordained in our own home parishes, a custom that was later accepted as the norm. The fact that we were ordained together as a group meant that our own immediate family were the only ones who could be present at the greatest day of our lives. What a lost opportunity! Thousands of staunch Catholics throughout our dioceses would never witness an ordination. Many years later, another bishop would start a different system. He would ordain priests in their home parishes. Sadly, by this time, the number of ordinands would already be dwindling.

My ordination day was typical of the pre-Vatican II Church. The atmosphere was one of very controlled, spiritual rejoicing - almost tinged with asceticism. Our parents, brothers and sisters had never once been invited into the College during our thirteen-year course. Now, even on the last day of this course, they were just to be tolerated! The 'distraction' to the rest of the four hundred students must be minimal. The fact that our parents had to be prepared to make a twenty- or thirty-mile journey to witness the ordination did not move the college authorities to provide a meal for them before they returned home. The bishop did not talk to them or even to us. How different from the present-day Catholic Church. John XXIII, do take a bow! Your Council taught us to enjoy our spiritual activities and not to be afraid to let it show. I'm sure that the Christian community of the first two centuries really enjoyed their 'parties' when they met to celebrate the early Eucharists. My present bishop, Ambrose, simply can't wait to mix with the people of the diocese on every occasion when they are gathered for any liturgical occasion. It could be a confirmation, it could be a now comparatively rare ordination, it could be a priest's funeral or some other celebration, but Ambrose never misses an opportunity.

On the day after my 25 July ordination, I celebrated my First Mass at St Cuthbert's Church in West Hartlepool. By this time my family were living in Middlesbrough. My father's work with the old London & North Eastern Railway demanded that he move house if he wanted promotion. Post-war food rationing was still in place so it had been necessary for my parents and sisters to make many sacrifices to provide a reception after my Mass. They had left no stone unturned to provide enough food for such an occasion. I suppose I was simply so overjoyed to be able to say my 'First Mass', that I never realized until later just how much work and sacrifice had gone into making the day the success it was. Like so many sacrifices made by the parents of priests in the 1940s and 1950s, we priests tended sometimes to be unaware of their depth. In those days, there were no Local Education Authority Grants. Our whole thirteen years of education had to be financed by our own parents and the diocese. This is why we had to 'sign on' for a particular diocese at the beginning of our long journey towards priesthood. This 'contract' included a promise of obedience to our bishop, as well as an ultimate promise of celibacy. Our eventual ordination was absolutely contingent on the acceptance of these two promises.

After the excitement of my first Mass, we were given to understand that we would have about four weeks holiday before we would receive a letter from our bishop informing us of our first parish of appointment.

One of the sacrifices undertaken by my sisters and parents was to rent a large furnished house in Drumcondra in Dublin for the month's holiday after ordination. Some family friends were to be part of that holiday and my close friend of my college days, Father George (Paddy) Dolan was to be one of them. After the food austerity of England during the war years and the immediate post-war years, Ireland was an 'oasis of plenty', at least as far as meat and dairy produce. Indeed, when I look back, food possibly played an inordinately important part in our lives in those very early years of priesthood. Even allowing

Ordination holiday - Drumcondra, Dublin -
Father George, Sister Pauline, a friend and the Author, 1948

for national rationing, the food regime during our thirteen years at Ushaw had been, by any standards, at best, spartan, at worst, a recipe for malnutrition. I suppose it was all part of the 'conditioning process' to which I have already referred. I certainly knew what it was to feel the very real pangs of hunger. Bread was our staple diet with a pat of butter supplied, which was about the size of the modern £1 coin. One of my most vivid and frequent memories was that of smuggling out of the refectory at breakfast time a large slice of dry white bread, for bread was always plentiful - the trouble was that your pat of butter didn't go very far. This slice of dry bread would be consumed ravenously during the study hour immediately preceding lunch. It would be helped down with a glass of cold water and occasionally, as a special luxury, with a packet of potato crisps. Crisps had just appeared on the market towards the end of the 1940s. This ploy would help to control the pangs of hunger and the noise of our empty tummy-rumbling. Thus we might be able to concentrate more readily on our Philosophy or Theology study notes.

A FORWARD-LOOKING PROFESSOR

One of the finest professors or lecturers in my later Ushaw years was Father Chris McGuire. He was a priest from Liverpool diocese on loan to Ushaw as a lecturer. In 1943 or 1944, Chris brought to his lectures on Physiology and Biology a modern dimension often lacking in the work of many of our other lecturers. His influence on me was such that, if I had lost my interest in bringing the 'Gospel message' to the masses in later life, I would surely have wanted to pursue a career in Medicine! Chris was always 'up to date', and was very much aware of what was actually happening in the world outside. Unlike some of his fellow professors, he thought it would be good for our training to share this knowledge with us. In the days long before political correctness became a constraint, he would emphasize the vagaries of heredity with a gem of a limerick:

There was a young lady called Sharkey
Who had an affair with a darkie;
The result of their sins
Was two sets of twins,
One white, one black, and two khaki.

I remember that for my year group he introduced an additional course on 'dietetics'. The world was just beginning to be aware of the links between vitamins, proteins, carbohydrates, calories etc. and the importance of regular exercise. On the basis of Chris McGuire's statistics we were able to work out that our average daily intake of calories would be *just sufficient* to keep a sick man comfortable in bed . . . provided he did not wander far from the bed to burn up any more calories. Like all my college professors, he is long since dead. Even in 1943 he struggled with what would now have been diagnosed as severe chronic asthma – at that time, Chris thought he had bronchitis! Despite his frequent fighting for breath between his jokes and lecturing gems, he was, nevertheless, a breath of fresh air in a philosophy and theology course which was often somewhat turgid.`

But where was I before I digressed? Yes, of course, I was on my first holiday as a priest in Dublin in 1948. I can remember Father Paddy and myself had discovered a lovely little hotel in Dublin called The Wicklow. It served unbelievable, beautiful, eight-ounce steaks – something we had only seen on films during the previous ten years. We made very regular trips to The Wicklow to build ourselves up for the parish tasks ahead, whatever they might be!

During our stay in Drumcondra we were occasionally visited by other college friends who had fallen in love with Ireland as a place for a holiday. We also felt a certain sense of recklessness, by enjoying the famous Abbey theatre or the Theatre Royal in Dublin. Because we were in Ireland, we were 'outside' the jurisdiction of the Westminster Synod Law which forbade priests to attend theatrical performances in England and Wales. Father Paddy had grown up with a love of Irish culture, humour and folk music. He had a fund of Irish stories and songs which were part of his Sunderland upbringing and which he sang with a very melodious, light baritone voice. One of my most lasting memories of our Drumcondra experience was Father Paddy doing the drying to my washing in the washing-up, after meals prepared by my mother on the occasions when we had not made a sortie to The Wicklow. My mother always delighted in hearing his rather roguish version of 'Courtin' in the Kitchen'. Father Paddy and I were to go to Ireland several more times, however, he continued to holiday there long after I had been 'seduced' by the attractions of the USA, but more about that later.

CHAPTER VII

FIRST APPOINTMENTS

After a delightful three weeks in Dublin, we returned to our respective homes to get ready for our first appointments as priests. Father Paddy was to be a curate at the Cathedral parish in Newcastle. I was to be a curate in a suburban parish at the north end of Darlington - St Thomas Aquinas. The difference in our two appointments was that Father Paddy was to be a curate, along with four other curates, in a large and busy parish in the very centre of Newcastle. I was to be the 'only' curate in a small parish in Darlington that clings to both sides of the Great North Road - at that time the main road between London and Edinburgh.

A curate's 'posting' or 'appointment' was then a very arbitrary thing. There were plenty of young priests available. In 1948 the bishop did not know his priests as well as he knows them today. Inevitably, sometimes the whole appointment process could have been something of a lottery. The bishop sent a letter of appointment telling you that you had to report for duty, usually on the Friday before you actually appeared in the parish church on the Sunday. In 1948, a curate had no say whatever in where he would go or to whom he would go. Indeed, I suspect that the parish priest did not have much say either in who was coming to him! The word 'consultation' had still to be invented in 1948. Inevitably, with such a system, there were bound to be 'misalignments' which often led to clashes of temperament. Neither the parish priest nor the curate had chosen the man who was to share the same roof with him twenty-four hours a day! The curate had promised obedience to his bishop and therefore, in those days, this presupposed obedience to the parish priest to whom the bishop had appointed him. In my curate days such obedience was 'blind obedience'. Many curates became aware very quickly that their 'conditioning' of the seminary days was very soon to be tested to its maximum. It would only be in the late 1960s that the spirit of the Vatican Council would gradually change 'blind obedience' into 'reasoned obedience'!

Most parish priests were good, holy men with a sense of mission and the desire to spread the Gospel message. However, before Vatican II, most of them were afraid of change. They must occasionally have found it hard to deal with the 'idealism' of a young, 25-year-old man, who was secretly harbouring thoughts of the 'Conversion of England'. There was a handful of parish priests who had already 'made a name for themselves' during our final college days. It was known that they were capable of 'breaking' curates. They were known to us as 'corkers'. Indeed, one such 'corker' actually achieved a top score of *thirty-two curates not out* during his innings as a parish priest!

Fortunately, none of my seven fellow ordinands were initially appointed to one of these difficult parish priests. One of them was *eventually* given such an appointment. However, by that time, the bishop was sometimes making a double appointment of curates to the same parish to try to lessen the impact on an individual curate! Sadly, from our 1997 vantage point, the system was quite wrong. A parish priest, who was not prepared to live harmoniously in the same house as a curate, should have been given a parish of his own, without a curate. But, of course, in 1948 very few parishes did not have at least one curate attached to the parish. At that time, the bishop had the power to appoint *ad nutum*, i.e. on the nod.

Happily, my parish priest at St Thomas Aquinas in Darlington in September 1948 was a kind and pastoral man. He was a Cork Man – an Irish priest, who had opted to work in England at his ordination, like scores of the parish priests in my diocese of Hexham and Newcastle. He had lost his curate some months before I was appointed there, a curate who had been 'on loan' to our diocese and had been recalled to his native Ireland. St Thomas's, I had heard, was a very pleasant parish, with a nice presbytery – or priests' house – and a newish church set in spacious grounds. I had also heard that Father Troy was a good parish priest who kept a good table, and was kind to his curates. Indeed, the omens were good for me!

ST THOMAS'S

I arrived at St Thomas's on the Friday afternoon. I had already sent my college trunk with most of my belongings by rail from Middlesbrough to Darlington. The bus actually passed St Thomas's Church as it completed the final part of the journey down the Great North Road, so it was very convenient. I rang the front door bell with some trepidation and excitement, and was later to learn that only the bishop used the large front door - everybody else used the side door, which was perfectly natural, for it was directly opposite the sacristy door of the church. The smiling face of the housekeeper, Margaret, beamed out a welcome to me. I was to be more fortunate than many of my curate friends in other parishes. Margaret showed me upstairs to a sitting room-cum-study. However, since I was the only curate, I also rated a small bedroom as well, at the back of the house. To me, this was absolute luxury - me, who had been used to multi-occupancy dormitories, and later to a small study, in my seminary days!

Father Troy was out in the parish visiting some sick people when I arrived and so it was not until teatime that we met. He was a broad-shouldered, thick-set man of about 5'9" with a mane of black wavy hair, slightly greying at the temples, a reddish complexion and smiling eyes; a handsome man in his early fifties. He moved slowly and deliberately. I learned later that he had been a great hurling player in his college days, however, his legs had lost their earlier spring and athleticism. He was to be the man who would guide me and mould me in my early efforts to 'save souls' in Darlington. In 1948, bringing the Gospel to the 'people of God' was simplistically known as 'saving souls' or 'working in the vineyard' of the Lord. Father Troy took my hand in a firm handshake and looked at me with that steady gaze and said, very simply, 'You're welcome to St Thomas's, Father'.

This was to mark the start of a typical parish priest-curate relationship of those times. At that time there was a huge gap between parish priests and curates. Curates were plentiful; they would have to be prepared to work a twenty-year apprenticeship before they, in their turn, would become parish priests in their own parishes. At the time of my ordination there were a number of parishes, usually in the larger towns, where there would be several curates living with a parish priest. Such parishes were regarded as prestigious by many parish priests. They would often become the preserve of older, experienced priests, although I suspect that Father Paddy Troy had never harboured any such ambitions. He was quite content to soldier on in a smaller parish of about 400 families, working with whatever curate the bishop might send him. The church and house were modern and debt-free, and the surroundings pleasant. Unemployment at the time in Darlington was nil. There was a serviceable parish hall in the grounds and a site for a primary school, but no actual school. Yes, Father Troy was very happy at St Thomas's. The question now was whether he could continue in that happy state, for he had never been sent a young man straight from college as a curate. Once previously he had been sent an older man who was a 'late vocation', a mature student to the priesthood who had worked earlier as an accountant. He didn't stay very long for the diocese suddenly realized that they had the professional expertise of an accountant at their disposal for £40 per year! Yes, that was the recognized salary of a curate at that time, and even well into the 1950s. Father Phillips - later Canon Phillips - began a long career as Diocesan Treasurer and put the finances of the diocese on a very healthy footing. This new curate, however, was very green and completely lacking in any professional qualifications at all. He was an Englishman, too! Father Troy had never had an English curate apart from Father Phillips. Most parish priest-curate relationships at that time were very formal. I always addressed my parish priest as 'Father' and he always addressed me, even in the house, as 'Father'. I was so anxious to please: I regarded him as the intermediary between the Lord and myself. He personified for me the will of God, and I tried hard to live up to this ideal. Now this may seem very strange to people reading about this fifty years afterwards, yet it is absolutely true. I can truthfully say that I never had a wrong word with Father Troy, although occasionally I had to bite my lip when he restrained my natural zeal. However, my very idealism must have put a considerable strain on him. Although I was extremely happy in St Thomas's, I never felt completely relaxed in this, my first curacy. I did hear Father Troy once say to one of his friends, 'I asked the bishop for a curate and he sent me a missioner!' I still wonder if he really was ready for a missioner at that time. Anyway, he had landed one. I was working in a parish where there was no school, no hospital, no institution at all. In the 1940s, 'systematic visitation' of the homes of the people was the foundation of priestly ministry. The saying 'a housegoing parson makes a churchgoing people' may have been coined in the Church of England, but it certainly was regarded as a golden rule in the Catholic Church of the North of England at that time.

I had been given a 'visiting book', a well-thumbed census book which had belonged to my predecessor, a Father O'Reilly who had returned to Ireland. It contained lists of streets and house numbers and family names, dotted with certain hieroglyphics, such as NT, HP etc. I couldn't wait to come to grips with the houses and the names listed in the census book. Ideally, at the time, most zealous priests would spend a couple of hours in the morning, and an hour or two in the early evening, just visiting families in their homes. These were the days before TV - *Neighbours, Coronation Street,* TV soaps - such distractions were unknown. Most married women would be at home most of the day. There was not a lot of female work in 1948, apart from shops, factories and office work which in any case was largely done by younger, unmarried women. Priests in parishes where there were schools and hospitals would have felt they were doing very well if they got round their 'districts', and worked through the census book even twice a year.

When I look back at my time in Darlington I know now that many of the people in their homes must have groaned and exclaimed, 'Oh God, not him again' as I loomed up at their doors! In the first full year, I must have visited every home half a dozen times. Admittedly, there were families who were always glad to see me, but there were many more who simply wanted to be left in their apathy; they certainly didn't want this spiritual 'Rambo' knocking at their door and reminding them that he hadn't seen them at Mass the previous Sunday.

Father Troy had not had any summer holiday, and he was looking forward to a break, to get away to Ireland. Once he was reasonably certain that I knew the boundaries of the parish and was able to locate the sick and housebound, he felt that he could leave me in charge. He had seen me 'Say Mass' and he was convinced of my zeal. He left for Ireland with some confidence - I was not nearly so confident, for I simply dreaded the prospect of a funeral occurring. What would I say to the bereaved? How would I handle a Requiem Mass and the cemetery? We had never had any practical, pastoral experience at all prior to our ordination, let alone dabbled in bereavement counselling. My thirteen years at Ushaw had been like a conveyor belt which had suddenly dumped me on 25 July 1948. Not only had we never been in an actual parish, but we had no training in inter-personal and communicative skills whatever. To make matters even worse, we had about as much maturity and worldly wisdom as the average fifteen-year-old in one of our present-day comprehensives!

Inevitably, the dreaded funeral occurred within twenty-four hours of Father Troy's departure, and in fact, within the week, I had three funerals in the parish. Somehow I survived and got through them, though my inadequacies were probably cruelly exposed. As a very young priest, maybe I had tried too hard to heal with words, and mumbled references to 'God's will is sometimes difficult to accept'. I soon learned the hard way - that it was best not to resort to words at all. I would learn to show my sympathy and empathy with body language - a hug, a look, or even just 'to hold' someone in their grief would say all that was necessary to be said initially. The time for words would come later, but it would only come when the bereaved were ready to make words part of their agenda.

MY FIRST SUPPLY OR LOCUM

There were twenty-eight priests working in and around Darlington in 1948. One of these priests was Father Tommy Murray. Along with a number of other priests he was a teacher at St Mary's Grammar School and was also chaplain to the Poor Clare nuns at Clare Abbey in Carmel Road. He was a good friend of my parish priest, Father Paddy Troy, who had promised him that I would say the early morning mass for the nuns at the Abbey for a few days while Father Murray had some well-deserved holiday. Now Clare Abbey is surrounded by high walls and entered by a very formidable-looking high gate. The gate itself is topped by dangerous looking spikes, intended to deter any would-be entrant from Carmel Road which is a ring road for the west of

Darlington. Now Father Tommy would normally gain entrance with his own key if the gate was locked. Unfortunately he had forgotten to tell the nuns that the new curate from St Thomas Aquinas would be saying the mass on the Monday morning.

Following Father Troy's directions perfectly, I arrived on my bicycle at about 6.15 a.m. in very good time for the 6.30 a.m. convent Mass, only to find the gate was locked. I knocked in vain for about ten minutes, and even tried one or two muffled shouts when there was nobody passing along Carmel Road. By now it was getting near to 6.30 a.m. and the nuns would be kneeling in their chapel about forty yards inside the walls, waiting for Mass! In sheer desperation, I finally decided I would have to scale the gate, spikes and all. I leaned my cycle against the gate, looked furtively up and down Carmel Road and as soon as the road was clear, I climbed onto the crossbar and saddle of my cycle. Somehow I hauled myself over the gate and the deadly spikes. It was just as well that my acrobatic prowess as a goalkeeper stood me in good stead, otherwise, I might easily have impaled myself on those spikes. The good sisters might have had to miss their Mass that morning. Many years later, in 1981, I told the story to the Mother Abbess, possibly the only survivor of those 1948 days. I told her of my first visit to Clare Abbey. She smiled an enigmatic smile, as Mother Abbesses are wont to do. Whether she really believed me I don't know; possibly she had forgotten, but then it was me who had braved the spikes, not her. She probably regarded them as unscalable. They are still there today.

CHAPTER VIII

MY FIRST VISIT TO DIPTON

It wasn't all work, of course. Saturday afternoons were always free from parish duties. My work in the confessional didn't begin until 6 p.m. and went on until 7.30 p.m. I was soon 'signed on' for the local Catholic football team, Darlington Celtic. One of the teacher-priests at St Mary's Grammar school, Father Vincent Shanley, knew of my ability as a goalkeeper and introduced me to the team for which he himself played. It was the start of an enjoyable season with them. Since they were not one of the top teams in Darlington, I got plenty of practise as a goalkeeper!

One of my very vivid memories of my time with them was the 'Universe Cup', or the Catholic Cup, played between various parish teams throughout the diocese at that time. A few parishes had maintained a stranglehold on the trophy for years: Hartlepool St Joseph's, Wingate St Mary's and Dipton St Patrick's especially. In the 1948-9 season, 'the Celtic' were drawn away in the First Round to Dipton St Patrick's who had been outstanding winners twice in the previous three years. I didn't even know where Dipton was - little did I know that I would eventually finish my years as a curate there in 1961-6. In the meantime, I had acquired a small, two-stroke motorbike: a green BSA Bantam. It was intended to enable me to get home to Middlesbrough on my day off without taking two or three buses. My uncle Bob, who was a bachelor and a comfortably-off metallurgist living in West Hartlepool, had financed the deal for me. Uncle Bob was my father's brother; he was keen on sport and more or less adopted me, recreation-wise, with the full assent of my father. Sadly, my father worked long and unsocial hours. He did not have much interest in football, but was delighted if he knew that I had gone to see Hartlepool United with Uncle Bob, but more about my father and Uncle Bob later.

I said we had been drawn against Dipton St Patrick's in the Universe Cup. I found my way up the thousand-foot climb to Pontop Pike, where Dipton straddled the nearby hills. I used my BSA Bantam as I could not ride on the special Celtic coach because I had to get back to Darlington in time for Saturday night confessions at 6 p.m. The rest of the team and their supporters were to stay on in Dipton after the match as it was customary for the home team to put on a tea and social evening for the visitors after the game. I was already changed underneath my motorbike gear in case I had to take the field very quickly - indeed, I had only to put on my football boots. I arrived just minutes before the scheduled kick-off and I took the field amid curious stares from the large crowd of Dipton supporters. I think they could hardly believe that the young man limbering up in the Celtic goal was a priest, confident in the knowledge that their team were the present cup-holders. They knew also that on that day it was strengthened by the inclusion of three or four players from the Northern League and the North-Eastern League, which were semi-professional leagues. They had never heard of Darlington Celtic, nor had they heard about this strange priest who was in goal for them.

The game was soon underway. It was played on an enclosed ground used by White-Lee-Head Rangers. Imagine the crowd's amazement, when, after Dipton had dominated the game in the opening minutes, the priest in the green jersey somehow, incredibly, managed to turn a goal-bound shot from Dipton left winger Charlie Errington around the post. The crowd were already shouting 'Goal!' Obviously it was mainly a Catholic crowd and some would have liked to have applauded the priest, but as the game went on this priest was preventing their invincible team taking an early lead. That early 'save' got the adrenalin flowing for me; I simply could do nothing wrong. I had some very sound defenders in front of me, especially Vin Saxton and Albert Gunnell. We somehow continued to defy the St Patrick's attack, even though they had 70 per cent of the play. A good goalkeeper needs luck as well as ability, and even though I played a blinder that day, I also had considerable luck. We finished up with an unbelievable 1-1 draw. At the final whistle I had to rush to the sideline, jump on my motorbike, football boots and all, and after hastily throwing on my overcoat on

Caricature - Darlington FC

top of my muddy green jersey, I sped away with a wave to the crowd! Soon I was flashing down Burnhope Hill back to the 6 p.m. confessional date I had to keep in Darlington. I never had the chance even to say anything, either to my opponents or to anyone in the crowd. Later on I was told by some of my friends and team mates, who had been very liberally entertained after the match by the St Patrick's people, that they couldn't believe I was a priest! Some even threatened to consult the Northern Catholic Calendar, and check on Darlington St Thomas Aquinas to see if I was actually listed there!

But worse was to follow for the Dipton supporters. The replay was scheduled for the following Saturday. Now Darlington Celtic did not have an 'enclosed ground' and so the replay would have to be played once again back at Dipton. Father Troy, my parish priest, was going away on the Monday and there was a wedding arranged for the following Saturday afternoon. Consequently I was not available for the replay. My substitute was a young 16-year-old goalkeeper from my own parish, a boy called Johnny Morrigan, who had been playing some great games for Beechwood Juniors in the Darlington Junior League. However, this time the Dipton team were to be without several of their star players. Although four of their players had forfeited their 'expenses' the previous Saturday with their own teams in the North-Eastern League and Northern League, their teams were not prepared to let them away for two Saturdays running. The replay result was Dipton 2 Darlington Celtic 4, and Dipton had failed in their efforts to win the Universe Cup two years in succession.

You might have guessed it . . . yes, the young goalkeeper in the visitors' goal was also to play a blinder that day! At the social evening in Dipton that night, the word went around that Johnny Morrigan too was studying to be a priest!

It would be fifteen years before Dipton St Patrick's would again win the Universe Cup. By that time, the mystery priest who had defied them in 1948-9 as a visiting goalkeeper would be their curate. He would play, coach, manage and cajole a new team. Ironically, he would be helped in 1961 by some of the 'stars' who had remembered him as the priest-goalkeeper of 1949, the priest-goalkeeper who appeared for two hours at White-Lee-Head Park on that winter day and then disappeared equally mysteriously on the green motorbike!

DARLINGTON YOUTH

Meanwhile, parish work went on as usual. Soon, I was busy trying to organize the young people of the parish into some kind of flexible youth club. We had a serviceable and well-used parish hall. In 1949 Catholic youth clubs were concerned much more with seventeen to eighteen-year-olds than with children. There was already an excellent young adult mixed club in the centre of Darlington which was well run and provided the opportunity for young, mature adults to meet. Some of the very sound marriages resulting from that early club were still in evidence in the Darlington that I would know in the 1980s, like Joe and Theresa Dolan. I tried to create a club in St Thomas Aquinas on a similar level, but although we had an excellent response from the girls of the parish, they rather outnumbered the boys. However, there were a number of older girls who were very interested in having a drama group.

I remember that we staged a play whose action took place largely in a convent which gave more scope for the female parts. The play was a highly colourful insight into convent life, and despite my efforts to 'damp down' some of the natural glamour on stage, the play was very convincing. I remember that one girl called 'Phil' really looked the part as an attractive nun. Her good-looking friend Joan, with her long blonde hair, was also very convincing as the girl with everything going for her, who was turning her back on the world to be a postulant in the convent. There were some excellent press photos from the local paper which went into my photo album.

Nearly forty years later, 'Sister Phil' or rather, her double, appeared in an Australian TV serial about nuns in a convent there. The resemblance was so uncanny, it was almost unnerving! I couldn't resist the temptation, found Phil's telephone number from one of her grandchildren who was at Carmel School and I told her to look at the next episode, especially if she still had the photos from the 1950 play among her memorabilia. She told me that she had already been alerted to the series by one of her 1950 contemporaries.

Ceilidhs were very popular at that time and we had regular dances provided by John Buckle and his music. One of our parish girls, called Teresa Murphy, was a brilliant Irish dancer. Her dark beauty and athleticism made her a much sought-after performer on the Darlington concert scene.

In 1949 concerts, whist drives and fayres were the bread and butter of parish fund-raising. We had no primary school, and we needed one, hence the fund-raising. Most of our young Catholic children piled onto a 'trackless tram' or trolley bus, every day. They were taken under the auspices of the Legion of Mary ladies, two and a half miles around the town to a Catholic school on Albert Hill called St William's. If we could raise a mere twenty-five shillings or so from a social, that was a very welcome effort as far as Father Troy was concerned. Soon, he was to find that his new curate would prove to be an entrepreneur in running parish football pools, about which more later.

I have mentioned St William's school. I can't resist telling you a true story connected with it. There were sixty-five or so of our children being educated there, consequently, four or five times a year Father Troy and I would go over to St William's Church. Father Cunningham, the parish priest there, and his curate, Father Tony Daly, would work with us to hear the two hundred or so children's confessions. One of these trips was arranged for September, a few days after the children had returned from their six weeks' summer holiday. Imagine me sitting in the confessional box, formally robed in cassock and cotta and stole. The priest can 'hear' the person confessing through a metal or wooden grille, but, because the grille is covered with a black cloth, he cannot 'see' who is confessing, nor can he himself be seen. After six weeks' summer holiday in 1949, a considerable number of children had missed Mass several times. Now Mass-missing on Sundays was at that time regarded as a very serious sin - a mortal sin, it was termed. That day there was a decided hard-core of children who had missed Mass every Sunday. 'Bless me, Father, for I have sinned . . . I have missed Mass six times.' Eventually, I thought I must take some sort of a stand.

The next child to come in to the confessional was a boy with a rather perky voice, who would have been about ten years of age. 'Bless me, Father, for I have sinned,' he chanted. 'Seven weeks since my last confession . . . I have missed Mass seven times.'

Pause for effect on my part. 'You missed Mass seven times?' I said incredulously to him.

'Yes, Father,' he immediately chipped in.

'What were you doing instead of going to Mass?' I asked.

'I was out playing,' he retorted without hesitation.

'Do you mean to tell me that you were out playing instead of going to Mass?

'Yes, Father.'

'Where would you have gone if you had been knocked down?' I ventured.

As quick as a flash, he retorted, 'To hospital, Father.'

I was speechless - he'd turned the tables on me completely. The fear of Hell was, in those days, a real aid to sorrow for sin, but it had never even registered with this unknown penitent. After my careful build-up, I was completely deflated. I suddenly saw the funny side of it and began to rock with silent laughter. I began to choke as I tried desperately to stifle the sound of the laughter. I could hear my young penitent shifting uneasily on the other side of the confessional, waiting for my words of absolution and his penance. I fought desperately to get control of myself for several seconds, before absolving him in a rather strangled, high voice. I'm sure he must have told his mother later in the day that he thought Father Caden was ill during the confessions.

CHAPTER IX

NOT REALLY ROBERT MITCHUM

As young priests fifty years ago, one of the things we had to do was pretend that we were rather more mature than we really were. At the age of twenty-seven I had never dated a girl or ever been alone with one. We had a youngish Catholic Women's League at St Thomas's. They very quickly discovered that they could easily make their young curate blush if they paid him some kind of sly compliment. Needless to say, some of them were liberal with their compliments and there were lots of blushes. I tried to become hardened to their efforts which, in turn, led some of the younger girls of the parish to rate me as a bit of a 'big-head'. I was beginning to learn the hard way, that my seminary training in preparation for celibacy left a lot to be desired.

I suppose I was vain enough to enjoy in a rather masochistic way much of the banter, especially after I had created for myself some kind of a defensive veneer against the compliments. Being a priest in those days did not give one much scope to be a snappy dresser. Black suits and large, very visible white plastic dog-collars were the accepted dress. In the winter months I covered these with a black trench coat rounded off with a black trilby which was possibly avant-garde priestly gear at that time. The 'detectives' of Robert Mitchum and Burt Lancaster were very popular at the time. Occasionally the teasing would encourage me to 'do' one of these characters . . . though, in truth, the resemblance might begin and end with the black trench coat, the trilby and the deep voice!

One incident, however, brought me down to earth, and very nearly brought someone else down to earth as well. One Saturday morning I was kneeling at the back of the church during Father Troy's 9 a.m. Mass. I had already said my Mass at 8.30 a.m. Near the end of his Mass, there was a crash behind me; one of the girls of the parish, called Kathleen, was there with her mother and she had fainted. Kathleen, although a lovely girl of nineteen, was certainly no 'size 10'. There were about ten ladies in the congregation that morning but no men, part from Father Troy finishing his Mass at the altar. I did not hesitate - I thought Mitchum or Lancaster in their films had always just moved over, picked up the unconscious girl effortlessly and carried her to safety. I was galvanized into action. Although I had difficulty in getting Kathleen into my arms initially, once I had got her there I was able to set off for the church door with her mother by my side. I walked with her rather proudly around the outside of the church, heading for the waiting room in the presbytery. By this time, Father Troy had finished his Mass, had walked out of the side door to meet me, and had opened the door of the presbytery ready for us. I was still a good twenty yards from the presbytery door; however, when I was halfway there Kathleen began to regain consciousness and began to roll rather dangerously in my arms. Suddenly she was becoming very heavy - I had already carried her for about forty yards. I was desperately holding on to her, my leaden arms aching and my fingers clutching wildly at anything to prevent her rolling away from me and falling to the ground. With a little guiding help from Father Troy and her mother, I somehow managed to keep her in my arms.

I eventually rather gratefully rolled her on to the drophead sofa we had in the waiting room of the presbytery, suddenly feeling very finite and human, and part of the 'real world'. After I had left St Thomas's I heard that Kathleen had married . . . she probably never knew how close she came to disaster, due to the over-confidence of a young priest who did not really know his own limitations.

ENTER FATHER TIM

Father Troy, my parish priest, continued to try to 'understand' me. He made allowances for my excessive zeal - I was convinced that the conversion of Darlington had really begun in a big way. The realization of this continually excited me. I suppose I am fortunate that this enjoyment of my work was not only there from the beginning, but

St Thomas Aquinas days - Darlington

actually continued right throughout my priestly years. I think it is a big bonus for a priest if he is happy in his work, and he is fortunate if he can continue to be so, despite setbacks and disappointments. It must be a very difficult and lonely life for any priest who no longer gets any satisfaction out of sharing the Good News of the Gospel with those around him. It can lead to depression and regret. This can be deepened if the task that he has been given by the bishop is made more difficult by the lack of response from those assigned to his care. Those assigned to my care in St Thomas's, Darlington were never lacking in such response. As a young and fairly out-going priest, on the whole, I suppose I appealed to them. My efforts to become accepted were, I think, fairly successful.

My priestly colleagues in the town were also very supportive. One priest who helped me, and always raised my spirits, was Father Tim Lynch, a close friend of Father Troy. Father Tim was working in a new parish at the Eastbourne end of Darlington. His church was a couple of temporary Nissen huts joined together to act as a place of worship. An unprepossessing, terraced house on the front street was his presbytery. He had a young curate called Father Goff-Bryce who was one of my contemporaries at Ushaw. Thoughtfully, Father Lynch would invite Father Troy and myself for lunch every second week, in order to give the two 'young priests' a chance to be together more frequently. Now, Father Lynch had a young, blonde housekeeper called Winnie who he would tease quite unmercifully whenever I arrived for lunch. He had the great knack of always keeping a really deadpan expression. He would chide poor Winnie as soon as she entered with the soup that 'We might get something worthwhile to eat today, now that Father Caden is here.' Winnie's blushes would trigger off my own blushes! However, underneath she knew that her excellent cooking was very much appreciated, not least by her deadpan boss.

Her deadpan boss indeed had a roguish sense of humour. He would often play jokes on Father Troy, and usually he could get away with it, even though Father Troy was himself much more strait-laced. I discovered that our priestly 'joker' played a trick on me which turned out to be very much a Catch 22 situation.

After thirteen years of isolation at Ushaw, Valentine's Day meant nothing to me at all. Father Troy had been so delighted that I had organized a very successful parish football pool, which had swept the town, that he wished to reward me, so he told me to go down to Burton's shop in the town centre and order myself a new suit. The proceeds of this parish football pool were quite phenomenal by any standards of that time. Quite frequently, a £100 profit was achieved on a weekly basis! The dream of a new infant school on the spacious site of the church was fast becoming a reality. However, I knew that Father Troy was constantly chuckling to himself at the thought that he had beaten 'Tim Lynch' to the launching of the parish pool. Indeed, I suspect he got almost as much pleasure from that realization as from his spiralling bank accounts. He insisted that I went to Burton's, where new suits made-to-measure were about £3. Apart from my ordination suit, I had never been measured for a suit. A stunning-looking young lady did the paperwork with me and directed one of the male salesmen to do the measuring . . . much to my relief! She told me she would inform me when it was ready, however, in the meantime, Father Lynch had gone to Burton's for a suit himself. He had been served by the same young lady who obviously knew him well as a regular customer. She had mentioned to him that the 'young priest from St Thomas's' had been in for a suit, and she had confided to him that there should be a law against men like him becoming priests. It was a few days before 14 February, Valentine's Day, and Father Tim saw his chance.

On 14 February I duly received a Valentine - quite an explicit one! I didn't dare tell Father Troy or anybody else about it. We had been invited to lunch at St Teresa's on Valentine's Day, and Father Lynch, deadpan as usual, cracked, 'I bet Father Caden got a few Valentines today.' The remark coincided with Winnie's entrance with the soup. Winnie blushed and I blushed, as usual. He then slipped in to Father Troy, 'There's a girl in Burton's who thinks your curate is a waste of a man.' Father Troy, aware of my embarrassment, told him to keep quiet and let me get on with my lunch. Father Lynch never referred to the Valentine again. When I picked up my suit at Burton's, I smiled enquiringly at 'the girl in Burton's', but she just gave me a dazzling smile back, which did nothing to answer my unspoken question. I wondered how much Father Lynch had confided to her about his intended joke. I daren't ask her - she might have thought me presumptuous! However, Father Troy did tell me much later that 'Lynch had nerve enough for anything' and quoted the Burton's incident. It was the only real Valentine card I can ever remember receiving.

PREACHING, AND ELLA FITZGERALD

My work completely absorbed me and Father Troy was very happy to delegate to me certain pastoral duties which he himself found difficult. Although he was good at what today we might term 'the sound bite' he was not particularly happy as a speech-maker or as a preacher. In those days there were no Sunday evening Masses. Instead, we would have something called Rosary, Sermon and Benediction. This was not obligatory and so we might only get sixty or seventy people on a Sunday night, compared with two hundred on a Sunday morning. The Sunday night sermon was quite a formal affair. People came looking for a worthwhile sermon. A worthwhile sermon in 1949 or 1950 was expected to be about twenty minutes or more. The week before I arrived in Darlington, Father Troy had announced that the new curate would give his first sermon next Sunday night. On the strength of this 'billing' there were eighty or ninety present on that first Sunday night to pass judgement on their new recruit! I must have done reasonably well because after that performance Father Troy decided that he himself could retire gracefully from the preaching scene. At first, he excused himself to his parishioners by saying that they must be tired of him after all these years. Later, he didn't even try to dissemble - he would just say, 'I'll do the Benediction, Father; I'm sure you have got something good for them tonight.' The next time he would preach on a Sunday night in my presence would be the Sunday night before I moved to Sunderland. I would be so 'choked up' at having to move that I would be in tears most of that day and couldn't face the people for my farewell sermon.

I have never been good at farewells. One of my all-time favourite records was one dating back to my later college days. Then, a young Ella Fitzgerald, at the purest height of her talent, could bring a lump to my throat anytime when she sang 'Everytime we say goodbye I die a little'. Throughout my life, Ella has haunted me with that melody whenever goodbyes were on the agenda. Several years after my ordination, I was thrilled to have the opportunity to see her in person at the City Hall, Newcastle, although I found her performance on that occasion an anti-climax. By that time she was a 'legend in her own lifetime'. Sadly, she indulged in far too much 'scat singing' instead of the pure melodies of her earlier years, and she never sang 'Everytime we say goodbye' at all!

However, back to preaching. Even though I did more than my fair share of preaching at Darlington and in the following nine years at Sunderland, I must say that I always regarded this as a great privilege rather than a burden. I sometimes think that my opportunities to take an active part in college stage productions broke the ice for me. They eventually gave me the confidence to face an audience, which in turn gave me that confidence to face a congregation. Such confidence would always depend on the knowledge that I was well prepared. If I had not been prepared, I would have shrunk from the occasion, just as a lack of rehearsal in a stage production would have filled me with apprehension.

CHAPTER X

A VISIT TO UNCLE FRANK

My mother was the youngest of fifteen children. By the time I was around, only five of these were surviving. My uncle Elliott Palmer and my Aunt Mabel, who lived in Bolton and Hartlepool, were in frequent contact with me right into the 1970s. However, two of my uncles, Albert and Frank, had emigrated to the USA as young adults to make their fortunes. Both had actually succeeded in this ambition in varying degrees. They had been the first of the fifteen children and consequently they were over twenty years older than my mother, their 'baby sister'. My Aunt Mabel, who was unmarried for the first fifty years of her life, had time to keep in touch with Albert and Frank, and so they were aware that they had a nephew who was studying to be a priest, a most unlikely scenario in their book.

In 1948 rationing was still with us in this country, and there were many things that were very hard to obtain. My Uncle Albert insisted that he would send my mother a priest's Mass vestment - a lace alb, for my ordination day. Sadly, eight months before my ordination, Uncle Albert died! However, before his death, he entrusted to his brother Frank the responsibility of sending the alb. Uncle Frank then began a correspondence with my mother, starting his first letter to her with 'My dear little baby sister'. Frank had always been regarded by his peers as a bit of a lad so he found it difficult to believe that the Palmer family had actually produced a real live 'Catholic priest'. He couldn't wait to see me in the flesh, and to see the baby sister who had been only a toddler forty-three years before when he had set out on his American adventure.

After I had been ordained a year, he sent the fare for a passage for me on the beautiful transatlantic liner *Queen Elizabeth*. My mother would go with me on what was to prove the most memorable holiday of my life. On the liner *Queen Elizabeth*, there were three classes of accommodation. There was First Class which was limited to royalty, film stars, occasional heads of state and millionaires. Next, there was Cabin Class which was for the very affluent who were looking more for peace and quiet on their voyage. Finally, there was Tourist Class which comprised most of the accommodation, and was used largely by the young and the fun-loving. Even though this was the third-rated class on board, it nevertheless had all the luxury of a five-star hotel. I had never seen such opulence - the sheer size of the ship was breathtaking. For most of the four and a half-day voyage, it was like being part of a small floating city. The ship was so huge and well-stabilized that it was hard to realize that one was actually at sea at all!

However, halfway across the Atlantic we were hit by the tail-end of a hurricane. I was very worried that my mother, who had a heart condition, would not be able to cope with the stormy weather. Towards the end of lunch I noted that all the dining-room portholes were being covered with their heavy metal covering discs. Within an hour this huge 'floating city' was being tossed about like a mere cork. Rather foolishly, I ventured up to a vantage point to see the storm. Soon, I was witnessing as a spectator the awesome power and fury of the ocean. Today, that memory is just as vivid as was the reality of the storm half a century ago. Quite suddenly, I began to feel queasy and started to stumble back down to our cabin. My mother was there already; she had gone below from the dining room as we had been advised to do. She was perfectly alright and showed no signs of being sick at all. Unfortunately, I did not cope nearly so well: within the hour, I was desperately ill. People had told me that there is nothing worse than a severe bout of seasickness: how right they were - I just wanted to die! My mother and our cabin steward were trying to help with ginger ale and dry biscuits, while I was just praying that they would go away and let me die alone.

As the huge ship lurched downwards, prior to hauling itself up again and out of the mountainous waves, there was a thunderous creaking and roaring noise. I was quite convinced that the next 'dive' would be the final one! Vividly, I could see the headlines in the English papers: '*Queen Elizabeth* founders in hurricane'. It went on for hours. My mother, whom I had worried about before the voyage, was never ill at all! Later, she had gone to dinner with the two charming American girls who shared our table. They obviously were good 'sailors' too! Immediately, they noticed my empty chair. They were in their early twenties and we had got on quite famously up to this point. One of them was a beautiful Jewish girl from South Orange, whose name was Lois. My mother, thinking that a visit from Lois would be conducive to my recovery, brought her down to the cabin, hoping that I would be feeling well enough to be cheered up by her. Alas, her beauty, charm and empathy were completely lost on me - I can only remember hoping desperately that she would go away and just leave me to die.

Eventually, I was on the road to recovery. I apologized for my apparent churlishness to Lois, and by the time we were sailing past the Statue of Liberty early the next morning, I was feeling fine. I was able to witness the - sometimes - tearful joy of Americans who were returning home. The Statue of Liberty symbolized for them all the nostalgia and dreams conjured up by their absence from their homeland for however long it had been.

Soon, we were through Customs and I came face-to-face with the uncle I had never seen. He was a sprightly seventy-year-old looking nowhere near his years and was full of jokes, smiles and half-controlled tears of delight as he embraced the little sister he had not seen since she was a child. I was amazed at the way he walked, at his whole bubbling personality: this man could have been *my* father! When we arrived at the Palmer home in Long Island there was a 'posse' of neighbours and relatives there to welcome us. Two flags flew from the flagpole in the garden, or the 'backyard' as the Americans like to call it. One was the Union Jack, the other was the Stars and Stripes. I can remember walking up the garden path and still feeling the movement of the ship under me, even though we had disembarked several hours earlier. Apart from the hurricane, I had hardly noticed the ship movement while we were still on board.

There followed a wonderful, but for me, too short a holiday. It was August and I had to return to the parish after three weeks away. Nearly two of the weeks would be spent on the sea voyages. Everybody tried to make my holiday something never to be forgotten. Uncle Frank and my cousins arranged a hectic programme for me since I would be leaving them in less than two weeks. My mother was going to stay for

Mother, Uncle Frank, Auntie Nellie and the Author - Long Island, 1950

three months with her long-lost brother. My cousins were very charming; they must have been a trifle overawed by my priesthood - they had clearly never spent much time in the company of priests. However, once they were convinced that I was not in the business of 'leading them in prayer' every day, they became more relaxed. As my 'humanity' began to overshadow my 'priestliness', the earlier awkwardness disappeared. My cousin, Lori, had spent much of the previous year very much in the limelight - she had won the title 'Miss Jones Beach'. She was a very 'poised' lady indeed and soon made light of my shyness and awe, and took every opportunity to tease me. Her brother, Fran, who was nineteen at the time, was working twelve-hour days as a joiner in the construction boom. Consequently I saw less of him than his sister.

Lori took us one day to Coney Island where there were some really 'scary' rides on the latest roller-coasters. On the most hair-raising of them all you could stay on for a second ride free. I had never experienced anything like it. My mother told me later that I was 'as white as a sheet'. Despite Lori's coaxing to stay on with her (quote) 'Come on, John, don't be chicken,' I resisted the temptation. My manly pride decidedly tempered by the certainty that another ten seconds on that ride, and I would have been 'throwing up' over my delectable cousin! We went bathing on Jones's Beach several times - Lori, as the reigning 'Miss Jones Beach', got a great deal of attention and not a few wolf whistles. Mixed bathing of any kind had never been part of my seminary training, so at first I tried to pretend that my beauty queen cousin was not with me; I would slink out of the limelight. But Lori would have none of it, going out of her way to give me confidence. She made it clear to everybody around that she was very proud of her rather gauche, Limey cousin. Psychologically, Jones Beach did more to dispel my almost phobic shyness and stifled sexuality than any other experience in my early priesthood. My training had undoubtedly conditioned me to equate 'sexuality' with 'guilt'. Such a training was to prove at best, inadequate, at worst, disastrous, for many priests of my vintage.

I have told you that Uncle Albert had died eight months before my ordination. However, he had a daughter and a granddaughter surviving him. They lived well north of Long Island and we had one really lovely day with them. Albert's daughter, Mary Reiker, was, of course, my mother's age and a widow. She was a warm, friendly person and in no time at all I felt completely at ease with her. She had kept up her religion well and was not in the least overawed at having a cousin a priest. Her daughter, Mary, was only fourteen at that time and was quite uninhibited with me. Once she had discovered that I was athletic, she couldn't wait to impress me with her ability to do hand-stands and walk on her hands.

Indeed, my earliest photo of Mary Reiker Jr. was of her standing on her hands, rather than on her feet! That day, she was wearing tartan slacks, so she probably felt even less inhibited because of that. The next time I would see Mary she would be Mary Hornbeek and she would be visiting my mother and sisters in Leigh-on-Sea, with her husband. Her two children, Durland and Alison, I would meet later on a future American trip.

THE ASSUMPTION

There are two other vivid memories I have of my stay on Long Island. I helped out at the local church on the Saturday prior to the Feast of the Assumption on 15 August, particularly with the confessions. Nellie, Uncle Frank's wife, went to confession frequently, and was therefore used to it. Uncle Frank was probably at best a 'once-a-year man'. The parish priest had left his confessional box to keep an appointment in the parish office, and had asked me to sit in there while he was out. Nellie bowled into the confessional box and soon discovered it was her priestly nephew on the other side of the confessional grille. She was surprised but not unduly overcome by the experience and left the box with a deadpan, pious expression. She did not, however, warn Frank that it was not the parish priest on the other side. Frank started the confession uncertainly, but was completely flabbergasted and thrown, when he heard the familiar English voice prompting him. I said earlier that Frank was a loquacious, bubbling, extrovert character - he had probably never been lost for words in his life - but this time was the first time. For the next three days Nellie never stopped chuckling at the trick she had successfully played on him.

On the Feast Day itself, I was allocated the twelve noon Mass. In 1950, Catholics were required to fast from the previous midnight before receiving Holy Communion and were not even allowed a drink of water. I well remember that 15 August. It was very hot - 90 degrees from very early morning! I couldn't sleep for the heat and from 6.30 a.m. I was trying to fight off hunger, thirst and a headache prior to the midday Mass. How I ever got through that Mass, which was a High Mass with singing and therefore longer than usual, I will never know.

CHAPTER XI

THE MAURETANIA

But the time passed so quickly that my first two weeks in America were over in what seemed like a moment and all too soon it was time for me to say goodbye. Even though there was no Ella Fitzgerald music, my heart went cold at this goodbye: to say that 'I died a little' was a gross understatement! Uncle Frank, a New York policeman nephew of his and my mother were there to wave me off on the *Mauretania.* I was sure I would never see Frank again although my mother was staying on with him for another three months. They came aboard with me, pretending to be interested in my cabin and the famous old ship itself. But soon the loudspeaker was calling out 'All those not sailing, please go ashore.' I shook hands with my policeman-cousin, kissed my mother and then it was Uncle Frank's turn – I turned my eyes away from his, realizing that he was thinking exactly what I was thinking. We clung to each other in a fierce hug for several seconds, fighting to control the tears, and then he was gone. He never looked back and we were never to see each other again. My mother told me later it was heart-rending for her to witness that farewell. He had asked me earlier to 'stay below' and not stand waving goodbye from the ship – I kept my promise. Indeed, I did not venture up from my cabin for an hour or more; by that time, it was already getting dark, but my heart was heavy as I tried to choke back the tears.

However, there were two things to be done. I had to find a steward to arrange to 'say Mass' the next morning. I had to find out which sitting I was on in the restaurant, and also which table. There were two sittings at all meals on the *Mauretania.* It had a smaller tourist-class restaurant than the *Queen Elizabeth.* Indeed, it was generally a smaller and more intimate ship, even though it also had its three grades of accommodation just as the 'Queen' had. I located my steward, who was a staunch Catholic from Boston. There were well over fifty priests aboard on that particular crossing. Since this was prior to the Vatican Council, and before concelebration was allowed, each priest who wished to say Mass had to be accommodated separately before breakfast in one or other of the lounges or public rooms, where a temporary altar or table would be converted for that purpose. My friendly steward had arranged for me to say Mass in the Cinema at 8 a.m. I went below to my cabin at about 10 p.m. without saying a single word to anyone for I was feeling desperately low. The muffled blast of the ship's buzzer as the *Mauretania* threaded its way through the estuary traffic guided by its tugs, only reminded me that we were getting further and further away from the American shore. I tried not to think of Frank and my mother back in the smart, wooden dormer-villa on Long Island. But the more I tried to shut out the scene from my mind, the more it crowded in.

There were four berths in my cabin, but no one else was there. I climbed into one of the upper berths and I tried to sleep, but without success. It seemed like hours had passed by and I was dozing fitfully when the cabin door crashed open. An unsteady figure groped for one of the lower berths and half-fell into it, muttering to himself. He was clearly too drunk even to think about undressing, and within minutes, he was snoring stentoriously. I was now fully awake but conversation was out of the question. Even when I tried to attract my cabin-mate's attention with a polite shout, it had not the slightest effect - he was dead to the world.

The rest of the night was a complete nightmare. Occasionally, I would begin to doze, but the dozing was always interrupted by a fresh bout of snoring and snuffling. At about 6 a.m., I could take no more. I clambered down from my berth, feeling completely shattered, left the cabin to take a shower and have a shave, and filled in the time until Mass reading some periodicals in the nearby library. Well before 8 a.m., I was in the cinema getting ready for my Mass. My friendly steward had everything prepared for me and served my Mass himself, impressing me with the quality of his Latin responses. He sympathized with me on my lack of sleep, and told me there were one or two empty cabins - it would be easy to separate me from my hard-drinking, hard-snoring friend. He knew I was on the second sitting at breakfast and he promised me that he would 'reserve' a chaise-longue for me on deck. He confided to me that 'By the time the second-sitting people got up on deck on the first morning, most of the best places had already gone. Just look out for me when you come up the main stairway onto the sun deck,' he said, 'and I will have a place for you, Father.'

Breakfast over, I went below and changed from my priest's clothes into a pair of slacks and a white tennis shirt. No sign of my companion of the previous night. I didn't even know what he looked like as it had been dark when he burst in to the cabin and when I had left to say my Mass earlier that morning. I made for the sun deck armed with my breviary - a black, leather-bound, very noticeable priest's prayer book - a constant companion of most priests forty years ago. The breviary was intended to be the instrument of a continual chain of prayer worldwide. At that time it was all in Latin, and even though it could be broken up into seven parts, it could take the best part of an hour to complete it - hence the habit of many priests in carrying it with them. Even on holiday, or on a train, or a bus, or a plane, it would receive some attention. In my Ushaw days, it was jokingly referred to as 'The Wife'.

On arriving at the top of the main stairway leading onto the sun deck, I was immediately spotted by my steward friend. He gave me a warm smile and waved me over to him. 'I've got just the place for you, Father. Come with me.' I followed him to what was the central part of the sun deck where he beckoned me to a row of empty chaise-longues, with two black-robed nuns sitting at the end of the row. As I followed him, my heart sank for I was already feeling very unsociable. I had harboured ideas of keeping completely to myself for the whole of the four and a half days of the voyage as I had been trying in vain to come to terms with the separation from Long Island and its wonderful memories. All I needed now, I told myself, was to be 'taken over' by two strange nuns for the rest of the voyage. In my later life, I was to make some very deep friendships with nuns - some of these friendships would provide strength for me throughout my whole priesthood. I hope Sister Mary Peter of Sunderland and other life-long friends will forgive my fickleness. The truth is that I was feeling desperately full of self-pity. My steward looked back and stated triumphantly, 'You'll be alright with the good sisters, Father.' I made a despairing attempt to 'disarm' him by suggesting that there was some space further over, but he told me that 'further over' got all the smuts from the four funnels, which could ruin a silk shirt in minutes. In my hesitancy, I was sure that I had noticed a look of doubt cloud the features of this staunch, Catholic steward, who could say the Latin of the Mass as well as I could. It was a look of mingled shock and even disedification. It seemed to spell out an unspoken question: What kind of a priest *is* this English guy who doesn't want to be talking to a couple of American sisters?

In a flash, I made my decision. I was in danger of disedifying this simple soul and must test his faith no further. I smiled and mumbled something about not wishing to intrude as he pulled out for me one of the vacant chairs near to the good sisters, and I thanked him profusely. I lowered myself into my chaise-longue, opened my breviary and started to say my 'Office', i.e. to recite my daily priestly prayer. Obviously the black, bulky, leather-bound breviary was an instant giveaway, despite the grey slacks and the white tennis shirt. The two nuns at the end of the row had 'diagnosed' me immediately!

I continued my silent prayer for about twenty minutes, however, I was rather distracted by a deck-tennis game that was in full swing about six or seven yards in front of me. A group of brightly-clad girls about twenty years of age were laughing and cheering as two of their number were battling it out on the court. The athleticism of the players fully matched the enjoyment of the spectators, I had noticed.

I had no sooner closed my prayer book than one of the sisters called over to me, 'Hello Father; it is Father isn't it?' I answered that it was. Encouraged by this admission, they continued, 'Do you mind if we join you, Father?'

I said, 'Certainly, Sisters,' and immediately they moved across to the adjoining chairs. I told them who I was and that I was travelling alone back to England after my first visit to the United States. I told them about my visit to my uncle in Long Island and that I had left my mother behind with him.

They told me that they were Dominican Sisters from Rosary College in Chicago and that this was their first time on an ocean liner. Then they looked at one another in a questioning sort of way, and decided that they must risk it. The older sister confided to me that they had a serious problem and they wondered whether I could help. She continued, 'You see these ten empty chairs, Father . . . they belong to the group of girls over there on the deck-tennis court. They are third-year college girls from Rosary College in Chicago. They are on their way to do a European travel year, and we have to deliver them safely to our Dominican House at Freiburg University in Switzerland.' The poor nun was gaining confidence with every word as she continued her story. 'We had no idea that life on a liner would be like this. After we came aboard last night, we had lost most of the girls within an hour! We went down to our cabin and never slept a wink . . . we just prayed all night that they would be OK. All of these girls are from very affluent families and the College is responsible for them and their safety. They are good girls, but they are carefree twenty-year-olds who have never been on a large ship like the *Mauretania* before. We don't know what we can do to ensure their welfare and safety after we go down to our cabin at night.'

They both gave me an appealing look, and immediately the younger nun, whose name turned out to be Sister Loess, breathlessly took up the story, 'We were wondering, Father, since you are alone and have no commitments on the trip, whether you could act as chaplain to them during the voyage . . . maybe, you could say Mass for them in the mornings, and possibly keep an eye on them at night when we go below to say our night prayers.' They looked hard at me, their faces clouded with anxiety.

I felt deeply ashamed that I had actually contemplated trying to avoid them and said straight away, 'If you really think that I can be of any help, Sisters, I will be happy to include them in my daily Mass which takes place in the cinema at 8 a.m. Then, if I can help in any further way, I will be ready to give it a go.'

Upon this assurance from me, their expressions immediately brightened. It was as if a huge load had been suddenly lifted off their shoulders. They called out joyfully to the girls on the deck-tennis court, 'Bebe, Lolly, Dede, Dorothy, can you come over here a minute?' The girls came over and stood around our three chaise-longues. Bebe, who had been involved in the deck-tennis game, appeared to be the ringleader. She stood there, toying with the deck-tennis rubber ring. All eyes were on me as I half-sat up on my chaise-longue. 'This is Father John Caden, girls . . . he is a Catholic priest travelling back to

England . . . he has agreed to say Mass for you each day in the cinema at eight o'clock in the morning.'

They were all good Catholic girls from outstanding Catholic families, and they reacted to this very positively. 'That's very kind of you, Father, it will be a real privilege, we appreciate it.' Bebe then introduced to me all the girls by name. Bebe was small, very attractive and very Italian-looking, with an infectious personality and plenty of poise.

Once the introductions were complete, Sister Loess decided to throw in the second part of her plan. 'Also, girls, since we are going to have to leave you early most nights, we have asked Father John if he would mind chaperoning you each night. We will set you a "curfew" and Father will help you to observe it.' This second item on the menu was rather unexpected, and it did not meet with the same rapturous approval as the daily Mass suggestion. There was an awkward pause as Bebe looked at Dorothy and Dorothy looked at Dede . . . Finally, in sheer desperation, and to break the awkward silence, I addressed myself to Bebe, who was still holding the deck-tennis quoit. 'I see you have been trying to play deck-tennis there, Bebe.' I had hardly got the words out before Bebe and Dorothy lurched towards me and grabbed an arm each.

'Trying, did you say trying. Father?' Bebe challenged me. 'Do you think you could do any better, Father?'

I laughed as I cracked back to her that it would not be fair for an English *man* to play an American *woman*, but had hardly finished the words, when I was forcibly hauled out of the reclining chair and bundled onto the court by the whole crowd of them! Bebe, although small, was very athletic, which I had noticed while trying to say my office twenty minutes before. She was to be the champion of Rosary College in the forthcoming England v USA encounter.

Now I had played some deck-tennis on my journey out to the States in the *Queen Elizabeth*. My goalkeeping and tennis ability had stood me in very good stead. This, however, was different. This was to be an 'International': the honour of the Stars & Stripes was at stake as far as Bebe was concerned! She was a good player and there were to be no holds barred. In 1950 prominent red fingernails were fashionable for girls. It soon became obvious that Bebe was prepared to risk her nails as she leapt around like a panther, scooping up the flying ring from almost on the deck itself. Despite a pause in the match, while she repaired some fingernail damage, she scorned my invitation to call it an honourable draw and insisted on finishing the match. She was urged on by the shrieks and applause of her friends. I needed to call on all my physical reserves and use my longer reach eventually to emerge a narrow winner.

At the end of the game, she gave me a dazzling smile and held out her hand to shake mine with the words, 'For a Limey, Father, you're not bad' - I was accepted! Cheers and handshakes from all the other girls. It was the start of a wonderful four days for me and helped to dispel the desolation I had felt on leaving Frank and all my American friends. This encounter was to change the whole course of my social life as a priest. I have often thought back that my simple, yet instinctive decision not to disedify my Boston Catholic steward indirectly led to the formation of the deepest friendships I have made in my whole life.

I soon found that my Rosary College charges had been far more capable of looking after themselves than their nun-guardians had ever imagined. They already had the run of the whole ship. On that previous night - the first night aboard - the Purser and officers of Cabin Class, and even First Class, had invited them to a big party. No wonder that Sister Loess and Sister Aguila had failed to find them. Following the bargain the nuns had made with them, the girls repaid their confidence with a very positive response - they followed me in a crowd as though I were the Pied Piper. Because there were two sittings at all meals on the *Mauretania*, half the passengers would never see me dressed for dinner or other meals in my black tuxedo and my dog-collar, and they would wonder who this blond young man in the sports slacks and shirt really was, who was constantly surrounded by a bevy of beauty, and yet seemed quite unfazed by it all. At night, as soon as I mentioned 'curfew' the call would be passed round among the girls, 'Curfew, Father says curfew.' They had quickly taken into their group a travelling concert pianist and several other important passengers. In an age prior to TV and video, every night they would take over the main lounge with its grand piano. With the assistance of the concert pianist and other friends, they would entertain a huge crowd, taking on board all requests. This was the golden age of the big musical -

shows like *South Pacific*, *Oklahoma*, and *Annie Get Your Gun* were all the rage; folk music of many nations was also on the menu every night. Bebe's talent was not restricted to the deck-tennis court - she could do an excellent impression of Edith Piaf singing 'La Vie en Rose' and could also bring down the house with her rendering of 'One Hundred and One Pounds of Fun' as Honeybun from the show *South Pacific*.

On the final night of the cruise before we reached Cherbourg, we had the official ship's concert. On this occasion, however, the talents of the crew were enhanced and augmented by those of the concert pianist and the Rosary College squad . . . to say nothing of their 'chaplain' with his rendering of Paul Robeson's 'Ole Man River'. But it was all over too soon and we were berthing at Cherbourg prior to sailing for Southampton. The journey that I had dreaded as we left

The Mauretania - *nuns and charges*

New York had turned into an unforgettable experience. Sisters Loess and Aguila were leaving the ship at Cherbourg to take the overland trip to Fribourg in Switzerland with their charges. There were lots of tears and goodbyes and exchanges of addresses. There were expressions of extreme gratitude from Sister Loess and Sister Aguila . . . and promises that I would be given 'the freedom of Rosary College' when I returned to America.

There was an emphatic promise from Bebe Romano that she would visit my mother and sisters the following July before going to Ireland and returning to Chicago.

And suddenly they were gone. As the *Mauretania* inched out of Cherbourg to finish the last lap of the voyage to Southampton, she suddenly became the sedate 'old lady' that she really was. It would be only a year or two later that she would begin her final voyage and this time it would end in the scrapyard. Soon the famous four funnels would no longer grace the Atlantic.

But for me, the memory of the '*Mauretania*' would always remain very much alive.

CHAPTER XII

MY SUNDERLAND MINISTRY AND A REVEALING GOODBYE

I would spend another few months in Darlington before the happiness of my St Thomas Aquinas ministry would be rudely shattered.

It was customary to move curates frequently from one parish to another. Ostensibly, the idea was to give them a varied experience of different ministries. However, quite often, the moves took place because their parish priests had asked the bishop for a change of curate.

Father Dan O'Donovan, the parish priest of St Mary's in Sunderland, had intimated to the bishop that one of his curates, Father John (Ginger) Donnelly, would benefit from a move. Bishop McCormack decided that maybe it was time for Father Caden to move to a bigger parish with several curates so I received a letter from him stating that I would be expected to arrive in Sunderland in ten days' time.

I suppose, if a priest is happy in his first taste of priesthood, then that parish becomes his whole world. It is a tremendous wrench to be suddenly uprooted and transferred to another parish, however important or big that parish may be. I had loved every minute I had spent in Darlington. I had been happy in the presbytery, with the people, with my parish priest and my other priest-friends in Darlington. Suddenly it was all going to end and I was faced with a journey into the unknown.

I have told you already how I hate farewells. There was many a lump in the throat, and an occasional tear, during the next few days. I found it especially difficult to say goodbye to some people who had worked very closely with me during my time in Darlington. One such farewell was with someone who shall be nameless, but who had always been a trifle brash and offhand with me whenever our paths had crossed previously. This time, the tension was palpable. I stretched out a faltering hand to say goodbye, which was gently evaded - she gave me a goodbye kiss instead! It suddenly made me begin to realize what man-woman friendship was really all about.

However unbelievable it may appear to the 1990s generation, at the age of twenty-eight I had never really kissed a girl in my life. Suddenly, the Don Quixote challenge of celibacy took on an entirely new dimension. In my innocence I was suddenly overwhelmed with guilt! I can remember hurtling down to St Augustine's in the centre of the town on my motorbike. Full of shame, I sought out Father Peter Stanley and confessed my 'imagined' guilt to him. Father Stanley was a senior curate there - he had been a 'late vocation' to priesthood after working in the world, and he laughingly reassured me that all was not lost. Gently he explained to me that I would have to come to terms with my sexuality - it would always be very difficult, but it could actually be done if I worked at it.

On my final Sunday night Benediction at St Thomas's, Father Troy preached for only the second time in three years. I was too 'full' to speak and give my final sermon.

Father 'Ginger' Donnelly was a great character with a wonderful sense of humour and a very wry turn of phrase. He was quite happy to have a change of parish. He had not always seen eye-to-eye with Father Dan O'Donovan, the parish priest at St Mary's, Sunderland. Ginger had also been a fine footballer in his college days at Ushaw. On his first Sunday in Darlington, he 'opened' by telling the people that they should pray for me. He assured them that there was no garden or greenery in St Mary's - only a huge back yard adjoining the railway station tunnel. He cracked that 'St Mary's has made an "adjustment of the transfer fee" to get me to sign on there.' He assured them that I would still be able to play football, but only in the Sunderland Wednesday League. In St Mary's, confessions on Saturdays went on from 4 p.m. to 9 p.m. Saturday football was out.

Harry Metcalfe, the local Harrowgate Hill newsagent, whose wife Kathy was a prominent member of St Thomas's Catholic Women's League, took me through to St Mary's, Sunderland. Harry was one of a few people in Harrowgate Hill who *owned* a motor car. He drove me through to Sunderland on the Friday afternoon prior to my Saturday start there, but before we left, he insisted on giving me an RAF flying jacket that he had owned since his days in the RAF. He wanted it to be a token reminder of our friendship - more about that flying jacket later.

ST MARY'S - EARLY DAYS

Father Dan O'Donovan welcomed me with a rather limp handshake. He was in his fifties, had a fresh, rather pink complexion and white hair. He had been ordained for the Newcastle Diocese, but he had been educated at St Kieran's Seminary in Kilkenny. He had actually been ordained at Ushaw with one of my former professors, a Father Barney Payne. Father Dan was a Cork man, like Father Troy, and came from a place called Clonakilty. In due course, I met my three fellow curates. The eldest was Father Paddy Kerwick, who was waiting to get his own parish. The youngest was Father Connor Daly, who was 'on loan' from Ireland. St Mary's had always had a number of priests on loan from Ireland, stretching back over a period of several years, and it would continue to have such priests during the nine years I spent there.

I found it quite strange sitting at a very large dining room table with four other priests - shades of the days in the refectory at Ushaw! Meals tended to be very formal affairs; even tea at 5 p.m. was formal. Conversation had to be directed through the 'chair' - in this case, Father O'Donovan. If we were all together at a meal, Father Dan would occasionally 'float' some theological question for discussion - not, I might add, always with any great success. On the other hand he might introduce some matter to do with the parish or with the parishioners. Maybe he intended to discover whether his curates were attending to their various duties in a conscientious manner.

Father Paddy Kerwick, who regarded any such questioning as an intrusion, would frequently dissemble. He would rather obtusely pretend that he couldn't remember the names of the parishioners referred to by Father Dan, or couldn't identify them - more especially so if Father Dan had been 'straying' into his, Father Paddy's, district. The parish itself was divided into districts, mainly for pastoral and visitation purposes. Father Paddy's district covered the 'posh' end of the parish, while Father Dan tended to be somewhat 'selective' in his house visitation. He himself was not responsible for any individual district.

I must admit that meals at St Mary's were never very relaxed affairs. I suppose the intention was to bring the priests of the house together as often as possible and for as long as possible. Supper, like tea, was also a formal meal. One was supposed to sit there at table from 7.30 p.m. for as long as the conversation through the 'chair' would last. Father Dan was not too keen on his curates going out after supper, and he would sometimes be guilty of lengthening the 'supper talk' before he would eventually say Grace. When he did finally rise to say grace after meals, that was the signal for us to leave the dining room. Supper was actually quite a modest meal usually, and if it did not officially end until 8.30 or 8.45 p.m., it did not give us much time to go out and get back again - the front door, the only practical entrance to the house, was 'locked and chained' at 11 p.m.

MISS WALKER

This brings me quite naturally to the person whose job it was to put the chain on the door at 11 p.m. Miss Walker was her name. Miss Walker had spent most of her life working in a priest's house. She had been with Father Dan ever since he had come to St Mary's as parish priest many years before. In those halcyon days, being a housekeeper to a priest was regarded very much as a special vocation and there were certainly plenty of takers. The remuneration was usually derisory; but then, cooking and domestic work in the 1940s and 1950s was not well paid. It was nearly always done by ladies who were single and unattached. Many priests' housekeepers were happy to have the opportunity of working, because the presbytery gave them a secure home. They realized, too, that they could be 'serving God' by looking after the daily needs of the priests who were 'working for God'. Nevertheless, most of them, especially in presbyteries where there were curates, knew that curates came and went; however, they knew that the parish priest usually stayed. Naturally, their first loyalty would be to their parish priest. The Old Church rules suggested that housekeepers should be 'of advanced years' and indeed, most of them in my curate days, would have fitted very comfortably into that category! In those days, too, many parish priests could become very dependent on their housekeepers, especially if their housekeepers had other talents as well as cooking and cleaning. Painting, decorating, coping with the doorbell and the telephone, handling money - these were all bonuses. Needless to say, Father Dan had become completely dependent on Miss Walker.

Even by 1950 standards, Miss Walker was different. She was a quaint little lady who could have been no more than 4'11". She must have been pushing sixty but did not look it; her long, dark-brown hair was always plaited and taken up in a bun. I can never remember her wearing anything else but black ankle-length dresses, relieved only by the white apron and the white headdress reminiscent of the TV series *Upstairs, Downstairs.* She always wore a pair of gold-rimmed spectacles and for most of the time, was smiling. Only if she became suspicious about something, or was challenged, would the smile fade. Rarely did we challenge her!

She was known to us curates as 'Gert', but I never remember addressing her in nine years as anything other than 'Miss Walker'. I myself had a very good relationship with her, but this was more than could be said of some of the other curates. All groceries and food were *delivered* to the very large house that was St Mary's presbytery. Even in my early days there, she hated to go out shopping at all. However, when I arrived on the scene, she was confident that, because I was English and came from Hartlepool, I would be well equipped to negotiate in the covered market or at the fish shop or at the bakery, and consequently she coaxed me to take on these extra responsibilities. Aware that she had an almost pathological fear and dislike of being 'in the outside world' at all, as she called it, I was soon cajoled into reducing her journeys over the presbytery threshold virtually to nil. During my nine years at St Mary's, I never remember her taking a single day off, nor do I remember her ever missing a day's work through illness. A day's work for Gert lasted from six o'clock in the morning until two o'clock the following morning! She slept, or rather, retired to an attic in the higher part of the house. No priest had ever seen beyond that attic door. Most of her day, however, was spent in a large, rather bleak kitchen. She refused to let Father Dan have it more comfortably furnished, mainly, I think, because she was genuinely a very ascetic person and would not have money spent on her or on her quarters. She did not want any domestic help in the house at all. Even her niece, Mary, was not allowed to help in the 'waiting on' when there was a special lunch, since Mary was not prepared to wear an ankle-length dress for the occasion. No doubt at all, Gert was certainly one of the old school.

In no time at all the sheer volume and variety of the work in a downtown parish like St Mary's completely took me over. The trauma and the sadness of my sudden departure from Darlington were noticeably alleviated by the excitement of the many new and undreamt-of tasks that now flooded into my life at St Mary's. There was an all-age parish school; there was a very busy District General Hospital known as the Royal Infirmary; there was a plethora of societies, confraternities and church groups that required the weekly involvement of a priest; there was a Catholic Nurses' Guild that embraced all the hospitals of the Sunderland and Ryhope area, including a large psychiatric hospital at Cherry-Knowle; there was a fast-growing technical college, which soon boasted the most important pharmacy training centre in the North of England; there was a small group of youth, which simply cried out to be launched as a potentially huge and prestigious club; there were two convents of nuns to be served; and there was also a grammar school called St Aidan's, run by the Christian Brothers and a girls' grammar school, St Anthony's. The brothers had taken over the school from the Jesuits, and they often had to rely on St Mary's for chaplaincy.

Father Dan's zeal was very much centred on the church itself. He would take under the umbrella of St Mary's any group that required patronage. These groups could range from the Third Order of St Francis to the Legion of Mary and the Knights of St Columba. However, Father Dan, like so many parish priests who had three or four curates, would happily delegate the weekly care of such groups to one of his curates. During my ten years at St Mary's, I probably was designated far more than my fair share of such delegation, consequently, a twelve-hour working day became quite normal for me. My work was only relieved by my 'day off' which usually tended to be on a Wednesday.

Traditionally, most priests looked to Monday as their day off. I was constantly, therefore, 'on duty' for hospitals, schools, parish house-calls and attending to casual callers, from nine o'clock on Monday morning until late on Monday night. Father Dan would go out for a leisurely drive in his rather under-used car on most Mondays. Blanchland was a favourite venue for him with its lovely Lord Crewe Arms. The beauty of the countryside, later to become Derwent Reservoir country, and the 'high' of a dignified lunch at the Lord Crewe were the purple patches of the week for this simply pastor of souls. I swear, though, that he loved to slip back into St Mary's around 4 p.m. and find me 'out'. If the traffic had been heavy, or the weather had been bad, he would greet me on my return to the house with, 'God, Jack, who is on duty here?'

I might have been called out to hospital or parish; however, I soon learnt the importance of telling Miss Walker where I was going and she would tell him with great unction, 'Father Caden is out at the Royal Infirmary.'

Later on, when we were alone at tea, he would mellow a little, and would indulge in one of his most often-repeated statements, 'You see, Jack, this is a busy place. We need good men here and fit men.' You will notice that I had already got one rung higher on the priestly ladder - here in St Mary's, to the parish priest, it was 'Jack' and no longer 'Father' as I had always been in St Thomas Aquinas.

THE CONVENTS

An important part of the work at St Mary's was the chaplaincy of two convents in the parish. Normally, convents expect a daily morning Mass and little more, but the Sisters of Mercy in Sunderland had a very high profile in the education world. They were a teaching order of nuns, and in 1950 they had reached their zenith for their adjoining convents were powerhouses of education. A hundred or more sisters, who were all fully-qualified teachers, ranging from head teachers down to young nuns in their probationary year, lived together in community. On one of their sites - Somerleyton - they ran a prestigious girls' grammar school, St Anthony's Grammar School, it was called, and a Montessori Preparatory School. Sister Mary Gabriel, a brilliant historian, was the highly-qualified head of St Anthony's. Now, in 1997, we are quite familiar with the head teacher who has now to be a manager-administrator rather than a teacher. Sister Gabriel was fifty years before her time! No wonder that most of the parents in Sunderland made it a priority to get their girls into St Anthony's!

However, the majority of this hundred-strong brigade of sisters went out on a daily basis to eight or nine satellite schools in the surrounding parishes. Here, they worked as head teachers, deputy heads and as ordinary teachers. As one who has spent a lifetime in Education Management, I look back on the Sunderland Catholic School scene and I can conjure up immediately just what the 'ethos' of a Catholic school was really about. In the 1990s we strive in our Catholic comprehensives to convince ourselves that this rather nebulous term 'ethos' is still a reality; but only with varying degrees of success.

The sisters elected their Reverend Mother every few years. Mother Bernard and Mother Alphonsus were two completely disparate Reverend Mothers during my Sunderland years. Mother Bernard, I can well remember, on one occasion while she was on holiday at one of the Mercy Sisters satellite convents at Wolsingham, was very intrigued with the pipe of a young 'Val Doonican'. Val was a good friend of St Mary Peter and myself. We had gone out for a drive in Val's new car, and jokingly and rather irreverently Val passed the pipe over to Mother Bernard, saying, 'Go on, Mother, have a puff.' To our great surprise, she had her first and last taste of 'lady nicotine'.

Mother Alphonsus, the other Reverend Mother in my time, was the complete opposite of her counterpart, Mother Bernard. A larger-than-life woman, she was nicknamed by the younger nuns 'Mrs Power' - partly because of her size, and partly because of her family name. She would occasionally have to telephone to St Mary's at about 6.40 a.m. to inform me that 'No priest has arrived this morning to say Mass . . .' My bedroom was the nearest room to the ground floor phone - the only phone in the presbytery. Consequently, most out-of-hours phone calls from hospital, convent or wherever were left for me to answer. Once I had been roused from sleep and had stumbled down the stairs, it seemed pointless to go back to bed, and so I would attend to the job myself. There was a taxi rank at the nearby station courtyard which often proved a godsend to St Mary's curates in the early mornings.

ROOM AT THE TOP

Sister Mary Peter was the headmistress of St Mary's Girls' school - the boys' and girls' schools were housed in the same building, but were separately managed. It was a listed building, and is still there today as part of the emerging university scene. Sister Peter was, for me and for most other priests at St Mary's during her teaching days, the epitome of the perfect nun. Cultured, well-read, gentle, humorous yet full of empathy, she was a wonderful support, not only to me, but to all my fellow curates at St Mary's, as well as to her teaching staff. Father Leo Coughlin was a great friend of mine in the 1950s - the only other Ushaw priest I worked with during that period. Sister Peter took Leo under her wing from the start, and gave him life-long support well after his Sunderland days. Leo and I had a very similar sense of humour. Both of us were devotees of Damon Runyon, Peter Cheyney and P.G.Wodehouse, three of the most widely-read authors of the 1940s and 1950s. Sister Peter was never taken aback or in the least fazed by our irreverent joking. Leo was a great mimic and he could have people in convulsions of laughter with his impersonations of Father Dan, myself and many others.

In those days the cinema was allowed to priests, even though the theatre was forbidden. A very avant-garde, slightly erotic masterpiece called *Room at the Top* was winning Oscars at that time. Sister Peter had moved into a new study at the top of the stairs in St Mary's school. With typical 'Petrine' good taste, she had covered the windows at the top of the stairs with some diaphanous, light material to afford some privacy to herself and whoever might be with her. One of the popular advertising blurbs for *Room at the Top* on all the billboards was the open window of the room where femme fatale, Simone Signoret, weaved her spells on the hapless Lawrence Harvey, while its diaphanous curtains gently billowed out in the breeze. Sister Peter, of course, had never seen the film. She had, however, been given a gratuitous and unexpurgated account of the plot by Leo and myself! Despite some initial embarrassment at our christening of her room, she eventually came to terms with the fact that her new study at the top of the stairs would always be for us 'Room at the Top'. I don't think, though, that she ever shared the story with Father Dan.

I have listed earlier some of the varied and demanding duties that made my life at St Mary's not only exciting, but much more demanding than my work in Darlington. The Royal Infirmary, with its associated centre for the Catholic Nurses' Guild and its subsequent demands in lecturing in the Preliminary Training School (PTS) was a duty assigned to me in my first year by Father Dan. Although one of my colleagues, Father Peter Starrs, was responsible for the 'wards', in practice a Sick Call Book was kept near the phone in the presbytery. Any of the curates would be expected to respond to it in any emergency call that came. One day, as the priest responsible for the Catholic Nurses' Guild, I was summoned to the office of the matron - Miss Shaw. She told me she would expect me to visit the Nurses' Training School to lecture to each group. I was to explain to them what might be expected by the Catholic chaplain in his ministry in the Royal Infirmary. My first session was a trifle daunting but I soon found it very worthwhile. It gave me a contact, not only with the Catholic nurses, but with the other 80 per cent of nurses who were not Catholic. Despite the fact that the C of E chaplain rarely appeared at the Training School lectures, I continued with my own input. After a while I found myself being invited to lecture on behalf of the whole hospital chaplaincy, and I continued this conscientiously for my whole time in Sunderland. The 1970s and 1980s became the era of the full-time hospital chaplain, usually C of E, and the lecturing and care of the staff became one of his specific duties. However, in the 1950s, my care and interest in the training of the Royal Infirmary nurses gave me a good standing with all the nurses in a group, not only with the Catholic nurses. Barbara, Scott, Shirley Goldie, Linda Rice, Rayna Robinson and Olive Stephenson would all pop up in my life during the next forty years. I can remember interceding for one non-Catholic trainee nurse with Matron Shaw, and in fairness she gave her a second chance. It was a prophetic decision for Margaret Hodgson many years later became the Head of the Midwifery Department for the Sunderland Area hospitals. Margaret, who became a lifelong friend of mine, would be present in 1996 in Sedgefield when I celebrated a special Mass of Thanksgiving to mark my forty years service with the NHS.

ST MARY'S CLUB

At St Mary's, we had a rather convoluted, upstairs church hall and meeting place in an old building adjoining the church. I had to enter it several times a week for it was the centre for the running of the Parish Football Pool. I had inherited this job on the strength of my 'entrepreneurial' work at St Thomas's in Darlington. Even though I managed to increase the profit by persuading several more new agents to help, I never achieved the dizzy heights I had reached in Darlington - there was already too much competition from other Sunderland parishes. The Catholic Women's League would meet in the hall every Monday night and since I was the only priest 'on duty' on Mondays, visiting their meetings also became my responsibility. Mary White was their very able chairperson. Interestingly, many years later, her elder son, Desmond, would be ordained priest after his wife's death; he would serve the same 'Dipton St Pat's people' who had so enriched my life in the 1960s. The Knights of St Columba for the whole city would also expect my attentions every Sunday afternoon - another of the delegations of Father Dan.

These frequent visits upstairs to the hall gave me the idea that, with some hard work, it would be possible to transform it into quite a large and presentable Youth Club. I persuaded Father Dan that I could 'do up' the old hall - we would have a raffle to procure paint and I would rally together a committee of responsible young adults to help me. Once he was assured that there would be no cost to the parish, he gave me permission. I spent several weeks contacting the many young people who regularly worshipped in St Mary's and I was able to gather together a very useful group, containing painters, joiners etc. I resolved to pitch expectation and age-range high, remembering the success of the mature mixed club in the Darlington town centre a few years before. Eventually we were ready to start work. I borrowed a couple of sanding machines from the firm - Liverpool House - on Saturday afternoon, with the promise that I would return them by 8.30 a.m. on Monday morning. Ladders and other gear we already had. We were about to produce an excellent, newly-painted dance hall that would be able to cater for over a hundred users. The lads and girls on the committee gave up most of their weekend and the sanding machine operators worked all night on Sunday. The transformation that was achieved in those few days was incredible. Those generous workers gave the St Mary's Youth Club of the 1950s a wonderful start. The fifteen or so members of the group were all young adults and full of enthusiasm but sadly many of them are no longer with us. As I pen these lines, faces are crowding into my memory: Ronnie Steel, Paddy Hunter, Little Glen, Betty Brack and Tom Poolan, Raymond Witte and Molly Graham, Alan Shanks and brother Eddie, Brendan Connaughton and Mary, Syd Cook and Mary, Betty Nicholson and Agnes Smith - these were some of the pioneers. They were joined later by scores of others who are still so fresh in my mind. All through my priesthood I have been meeting outstanding Catholics who would warmly and enthusiastically remind me of those halcyon days!

They persuaded me to keep the age-grouping 'high'. We should aim at eighteen-year-olds as an average and should build up the numbers by word of mouth and by the grapevine.

Its success may seem incredible now in 1997, but remember that the idea of giving young Catholic people a real chance to meet socially on a regular basis, with a real band providing the music, was something quite untried before 1952. Moreover, there were no real counter-attractions and television was still in its infancy. We were able to form a first-class choir, football teams, and netball teams, as well as organizing club outings. Some of my older fellow priests thought that I had taken leave of my senses. Wasn't I deliberately throwing together girls and boys who had already started 'courting' or were about to do so? *My* thoughts were that if a Catholic boy had a non-Catholic girlfriend, or vice versa, we would encourage them to come to the club and we would make them welcome.

The 1950s was a very popular decade for converts and *many* resulted from St Mary's Club. The opportunity for Catholic marriages was actively being provided. I remember counting up well over a hundred Catholic marriages that I knew of myself; but there must have been many more that I was not aware of. The tentacles of St Mary's Club spread not only through the Sunderland parishes, but also far afield to places like Ryhope, Silksworth, Murton, Easington, Seaham, and to the north to places like Boldon. Such was the popularity of the club that we must have had well over 500 members on our books. Music was provided by Billy Graham and Paddy Fox who were excellent on piano and drums; they were occasionally reinforced by an accordion. While they slipped out for a pint over the road to the Grand Hotel in the intermission time, we would have a Top-Twenty record session for about twenty-five minutes. 'Rock Around The Clock' was one of the big hits at the time and I can well remember having to exercise special 'personal' control while Bill Haley rocked around.

I would have loved to have joined the lads with their heavy brogue footwear and their serious expressions. I often teased Bryan Taylour, Kevin Docherty, Tony Holyoake and Cranston McLeish . . . to let their faces 'slip' a little while they were busily gyrating. However, in the 1950s any priestly participation would have shocked the youngsters rigid. It was twenty years later when I finally really let myself go at a parish dance at Sedgefield Racecourse. By that time the wheel would have turned full circle - Bill Haley and 'Rock Around The Clock' would once again be in the charts!

Diffidence about their faith and peer pressure seemed to hold no place among the young Catholics in St Mary's Club, or certainly was never in evidence. Quite often, during the intermission time on Sunday nights, I would take a roving microphone and lead the floor in a discussion, fielding questions about the Church or religion. Father Leo (Coughlin) would masquerade as 'a lad about town', and would act as a devil's advocate. The reaction and behaviour of the young members was always impeccable. We had certain ground rules for the club and members responded by being 'responsible' at all times. I would again be involved in youth work later in my capacity as a county councillor in Sedgefield. It would be twenty years later but I would never again find the kind of response that I found from the young people in St Mary's Club, Sunderland.

Over the next forty years, these faces from the past would suddenly materialize in the most unexpected places - the Edie Rimmers, the Molly Carrahars and the Sybil Hewetts. Finally, at the Golden Jubilees of my friends Father Sam Mallaley and Father Tony Daley, I would meet up again with Tom Garton, my St Mary's MC, and with Belsy Smith and Joe Coyne, still enthusing about those St Mary's Club days.

CHAPTER XIII

THE RED SWEATER AND THE FLYING JACKET

The early 1950s was the infancy of Social Services. In a city parish like St Mary's, the priest had to be, in Saint Paul's words, 'All things to all men' - and to all women as well! Despite the contribution of the shipyards and factories to the Sunderland economy, there was still a lot of poverty and deprivation about. At the back of St Mary's Church, stretching as far as the Gill Bridge Avenue Police Station, right along the river, there was a dimly lit no-man's-land area. It was later demolished and was replaced by fashionable shops and a large chain store. However, in 1952 this area and another riverside area east of Sunderland High Street were very tough areas indeed. There was more than an average percentage of 'St Partick's Day Catholics' living there who rarely darkened the church more than once or twice a year. The police were shrewd enough not to intrude too much in these areas on Friday or Saturday nights. A discreet phone call to St Mary's would alert the priest that there was trouble. If the police themselves moved in it could end in a riot, but if the priest was prepared to take a walk down there, then who knows - a peaceful solution might be found. As successive curates between the 1930s and the 1950s made friends with some of the police inspectors, this was a formula that worked reasonably well. Many a Saturday night after the long confessions session, I would take a stroll to get a breath of air after being shut up in the confessional for nearly five hours. Later on, after Father Leo joined me as a fellow curate, he was quite fascinated by the whole scene. Telling the tale years later, he would shamelessly embellish it, saying that before he came to the 'big city' in 1953, he had been told about this Rambo-style curate, Father Jack Caden. He had been told that Father Jack would put on a big red sweater on Saturday nights and after sorting out a couple of fights in his district, he would then slip into The Rink - the mecca for the Saturday night dancing crowd.

Leo told the story to a packed church on the occasion of my forty years' priestly anniversary, and had the congregation, literally, falling about the benches. He did admit, however, that he never found the red sweater, despite the surreptitious search for it one day in my room.

The truth was, of course, well short of Father Leo's apocryphal stories, but nevertheless, truth is often stranger than fiction. There is one true story I might relate to you concerning the outsize airforce flying jacket that I was given by Harry Metcalfe before I left Darlington.

At one o'clock in the morning, and a very foggy winter morning it was, the doorbell of the presbytery rang loudly several times. As usual, due to the proximity of my room to the door, I was the only one who heard it. I stumbled to the door and on opening it, found a distraught woman in her thirties, with two young children. She had a coat on over her nightdress as did the frightened, shivering children.

I did not know her or the children. Hysterically and tearfully, she told me that her husband was a Catholic and had come home drunk and very late. He had tried to get 'his rights' as it was sometimes termed at the time. When she refused, he began to hit her and with the children now awake and crying, she had grabbed her coat and their coats, and had told him she was going for the priest. They lived in a two up-two down Dickensian cottage, joined to other similar styled dwellings by the side of the river. Dimly lit arched courtyards connected these dwellings by very narrow streets. The whole sixty yards-square area was obviously designated for slum clearance, but the Borough Council had not yet completed the rehousing of all the residents. What lighting there was came from old gas lighting.

I had no idea what manner of man her husband was, nor did I know the family, although it was part of my 'district'. Despite the knowledge that I was a fairly fit, twelve stones, 5'11" priest, I was obviously apprehensive - he might be much bigger than me. He was also in a mean mood and had been drinking; he might resent my interference. I signalled for her to wait quietly in the hallway of the presbytery while I pulled on some clothes. After slipping on my stockings, shoes and trousers, I then had a brainwave - I would wear the flying jacket instead of my coat! It would at least make me look much bigger and more powerful than I really was. We left the presbytery quietly - still not a sound from any of my colleagues in the upstairs rooms. In three or four minutes she was leading me into the 'maze' where she lived. It was dark and very foggy. The solitary gaslight in the courtyard glowed eerily. She now looked much calmer and happier, and the children's eyes were turned in my direction. There was an almost palpable silence. The mother took me to the bedroom door and said to me, rather confidently, 'He's in there, Father, now you go in and tell him.' The bedroom was in darkness - the only light getting in to it was from the now dimly-lit living room. I moved through the narrow doorway and was reassured as I felt the brush of the well-padded flying jacket against the lintels. My heart was beating fast but I knew I could not let the unfortunate woman down at this stage. I was comforted by the fact that, with the dim light behind me, I must have looked huge in the doorway. My eyes strained to see the figure in the bed. Gradually I could pick him out in the darkness as he shifted uneasily under the bedspread. I loomed nearer to him and said, 'What kind of a man are you to drive out your wife and bairns on a night like this? You ought to be ashamed of yourself.'

He obviously was not in any mood to leap up and attack me. I gained a little confidence as my proximity quickly sobered him up, and he mumbled something about being 'Sorry, Father, for the trouble.'

I bent over the bed, and with hindsight, rather recklessly, thought that I should make the lesson a lasting one. I grabbed a handful of candlewick bedspread and shirt, which he was pulling up over his chest, and half-lifted him out of the bedclothes. 'If you ever lay a finger on your wife again, I will give you the hiding of your life.'

'I won't, Father, I won't,' he stammered.

'O.K. then, don't have her come for me again. Goodnight now and God bless.'

I spotted him a few days later emerging from the courtyard and he saluted me rather sheepishly - he must have been all of 5'7" and could not have weighed much more than 9 stones! Needless to say, I never met him in the church - no doubt the family were rehoused several months later. I was never summoned again during the night. However, one of my fellow curates, Father Nelus Horan, was roused one night when I was on holiday. Prudently he told the good woman to go back home and put the children to bed - he would look into it in the morning. By the time I returned from holiday, the family had been rehoused in Thorney Close, a new estate to the west of Sunderland.

THE BIRTH OF THE CATHOLIC STAGE GUILD IN SUNDERLAND

I have already stated that any Catholic organization which was homeless and in need of a liturgical base, had an excellent chance of finding one if it approached Father Dan O'Donovan in the right way. The right way was to indicate that it could add something to the plethora of Church worship we already had in St Mary's. This is how we acquired at various times, the Legion of Mary, the Third Order of Saint Francis, the Children of Mary, the Guild of SS Cosmos and Damian, the Catholic Nurses' Guild and the Grail, to mention only a few! One other important organization, however, we acquired by 'Royal Command' or at any rate, by Westminster Command!

One lunchtime, just after we had finished our 'drop of good soup' as Miss Walker was wont to call it, Father Dan produced a letter which had arrived that morning from Archbishop's House, Westminster. It was addressed personally to Father Dan O'Donovan. Father Dan was not in the habit of receiving letters from the Cardinal, even if they had *only* been signed by him He did not invite his curates to read it, but allowed us to see its authenticity, by letting us see Cardinal Griffin's coat-of-arms clearly visible on the envelope, and 'Very Reverend Dean O'Donovan' printed equally clearly. He later became a canon but Father Dan liked nothing better than to be referred to as Dean O'Donovan as it had a ring about it. He then gave us the message from Westminster: 'The Cardinal wants us to set up the Catholic Stage Guild here in Sunderland.'

I'm sure that neither Father Dan nor my fellow curates, who were all Irish priests at the time, had ever heard of it. I had recently read about this very exclusive little group which was based in Maiden Lane in London, and which had an annual Mass attended by Eamonn Andrews, the Duke of Norfolk and one or two other prominent Catholics. It seemed mainly, however, to be a vehicle for asking God's blessing on Catholic performers and entertainers at a Mass once a year. Indeed, it had been just that, until the unlikely conversion of a variety artist originating from the north-east of England who was known as Wee Georgie Wood.

George had been a star for many years. He used to do a 'mother and badly-behaved son' act with a lady called Dolly Harmer. He had recently been received into the Church by the Cardinal, and had immediately challenged him that in thirty years on the stage, he had never been visited at the theatre by a Catholic priest. He told the cardinal that the Anglican Church had a network called 'The Actors' Church Union'. It had a network of chaplains all over the country. However, the Catholic Church, with its great heritage of home and family visitation, had completely ignored the theatre. To make matters worse, most performers at that time outside of London were always touring. Twice-nightly variety was the main form of entertainment in all the larger towns and cities. If an artist was working regularly, he or she would rarely be at home and could, in practice, only meet a priest while on tour. Doubtless, Cardinal Griffin had pointed out to 'Wee Georgie' that Catholic priests were forbidden by the Westminster Synod Law to attend any live theatrical performances, hence the dearth of priests at theatre stage doors. But Georgie was not to be side-tracked: he pestered him until he gave in. The Cardinal's secretary, in due course, did the necessary research, and sent out the batch of letters to senior parish priests in all the larger cities and towns where there was a prominent theatre. I suspect that the priest who had the main part in all this was later to become much more well known as Archbishop Derek Worlock of Liverpool. I have not, however, been able to verify this with complete certainty.

Nevertheless, Father Dan actually did receive a letter signed by Cardinal Griffin which was quite enough for a churchman as orthodox as Father Dan. 'God, we will have to do something about this,' he stated, 'now that the cardinal is asking us to do this, we will have to do it.' Silence from all at the table. Certainly, no immediate volunteers for the job. Father Dan looked round expectantly and his gaze seemed to linger in my direction. He had had three or four hours to think about it since the post had arrived that morning, and had rightly surmised that there would be no volunteers, so he would have to indicate himself who should take it on.

'God, Jack, I think that you would be the man for this,' he ventured. 'You seem to be able to talk to anyone. It's clear the Cardinal expects someone to do it, but God, now I would be too shy to do anything like this. But Jack, you are not shy. I'm sure you would be able to make a good job of it. I'm sure we would all help you in any way.'

So that was it! Father Dan rang the bell and Miss Walker brought in the main course, pushing 'the dumb waiter' as she called the wooden trolley which trundled in our meals. There were undisguised smiles of relief on the faces of my fellow curates, and attempts to change the conversation to safer topics than cardinals' letters!

At the end of lunch I was summoned to Father Dan's room where he emphasized the importance of the job I had just been given. The Westminster Secretariat had even supplied in the letter the name of the manager of the Empire Theatre, a Mr Jess Chalons. Such meticulous attention to detail also pointed - I write now with hindsight - to Father Derek Worlock! I promised Father Dan I would make an appointment with Jess Chalons as soon as possible and that I would keep him - Father Dan - informed. I secretly marvelled at the fact that Father Dan was actually encouraging me to take such an interest in the theatre. Normally he would have reacted with disapproval to any priestly interest in the cinema, let alone the theatre, regarding it as worldly and not wholesome for priests. But the fact that the letter had come from the Cardinal . . . that was enough!

Jess Chalons was delighted. He introduced me to the stage door man, a Mr Jack Knudsen, and told me I would be welcome in his office or backstage any time. He arranged for me to meet a Canon Ford of Christchurch, a C of E church in Sunderland, who was the Anglican Actors' Church Union chaplain. Canon Ford called into the theatre every Tuesday night, and I agreed with him that we would visit the artists on different nights so they would not get a surfeit of 'dog collars' on the same night. In due course, we were to work together on producing an exhaustive list of very good stage digs so that visiting performers would also be comfortable, even if there was a very large cast, as there would occasionally be with pantomimes or musicals. I put up on the stage door noticeboard the official card of the Catholic Stage Guild - also supplied in the cardinal's letter - with the times of

Masses, location of the church and the name and telephone number of the chaplain.

Wee Georgie had done his job well - we were ready for action . . .

CHAPTER XIV

THE DAILY ROUND

The ordinary priestly work went on as usual - the daily Masses, whether in the church or at one of the convents, the routine daily visitation of the homes of parishioners, the twice-weekly calls at the school, the frequent interviews with callers at the door, whether genuine ones or just 'knights of the road', as we called the daily half-dozen tramps and beggars. The latter were legion in their numbers and ranged from quiet young men to 'old lags' who had been on the road all their lives. The stories they told were fairly uniform - they usually involved a bus journey that was imperative or money for food. In nine years on the main street of Sunderland, I must have heard hundreds of similar stories and the occasional 'original' one that would elicit an extra pecuniary response. We used to increase the handout for the sheer ingenuity of the story. Barely did a day go by without our quota of beggars calling. This was long before the age of the 'Bobby Thompson Giro' so the numbers were much higher. Afternoon or evening callers would often want the price of a night's lodging at the Salvation Army Hostel near the docks in High Street East. I soon learnt that it was wiser for me to have an 'arrangement' with the Hostel Captain and to settle my account with him regularly, rather than handing out half-crowns willy-nilly! Sadly, I must say that in retrospect, four out of five of these callers were in dubious good faith at best for many of them preferred the life on the road. Some of them were still appearing regularly at the end of my nine years there. Indeed, I could write a book simply on my experiences with these 'knights of the road' of the 1950s, but the repetition of many of the stories might prove boring.

One of the main reasons for extra priests at St Mary's was that it was in Sunderland town centre. It provided extra opportunities for confessions therefore. In the 1950s most good Catholics would go to confession once a month, at least; many of them, young people included, would go even more frequently. Our Saturday confessions schedule at St Mary's would begin at 4 p.m. and continue often until 9 p.m. There would be a twenty-five minute break for a cup of tea at 5 p.m, although this would depend on whether one could 'escape' from the confessional box at all! At Christmas and Easter, scores of penitents formed queues outside individual confessional boxes. I was in a temporary box with curtains at the back of the church, and therefore it was more difficult for me to escape. As the priests down the side of the church, with their solid, room-like confessional boxes managed to escape if there was a pause after the door was closed, then the disappointed ones would quickly hurry to the back of the church, and crowd outside my box. Here they would hover outside the curtain and would be in, almost before the previous penitent had got properly out. Regularly, at Christmas and Easter, when the crowds were huge, I would get someone darting in and beginning, 'Bless me, Father, for I have sinned . . . I lost my temper while waiting for confession, because somebody jumped the queue.'

Most Saturday nights, I would hear about one hundred confessions, often more. This number, multiplied by the work of other confessors hearing as well, would mean a total of five hundred or so confessions every Saturday in the church. I reckoned that only about ten out of every hundred were voices that would be known to us. At least 90 per cent were Catholics from up to a ten-mile radius of St Mary's who wanted to ensure complete anonymity in their confession.

Looking back, was it the golden age of the Church? There are conflicting views on this to this day. Comedian, Billy Connolly, often 'cracked' that he was brought up as a Catholic and had managed an A level in guilt! Prior to 1965, emphasis was on sin rather than on perfection and the love of God. The Second Vatican Council referred to earlier certainly changed this emphasis for ever. It made Catholics take responsibility according to their individual consciences for their own morality, especially in matters of sexuality and human weakness.

Prior to Vatican II, Catholics thought of God much more as a God who would 'get them' if they transgressed, rather than a God who loved them despite their transgressions. Maybe the pendulum has swung too much the other way . . . I don't know. The cold fact, however, remains that in the St Mary's of the 1990s, a single priest deals with about fifty confessions as a maximum on a busy Saturday. The days of five hundred every Saturday are just a story that must seem quite incredible to the pupils of St Anthony's or St Aidan's Comprehensive Schools in Sunderland, as their grandparents try to impress them.

The old Latin 'Tridentine' Mass has gone, maybe for ever. The rather baroque-style choir of St Mary's is just a memory. Gerry Cunmingham, its conductor in my time there, has recently become a Benedictine monk, after the sad death of his wife. The polyphony of the weekly Sunday High Mass, with deacon and sub-deacon, has just become a story that is told by one or two elderly parishioners. They could tell the story, too, of an 'ethereal experience' at one of the Easter midnight masses . . . Easter midnight masses that never really caught on and soon disappeared.

SADLERS WELLS INTERLUDE

The Sadlers Wells Opera Company had been performing at the Empire during Holy Week. I had arranged rehearsal facilities in St Mary's Hall for them with their musical director. As a token of gratitude, he told me that some of the cast would come down to the church on Good Friday morning and also for midnight mass on Holy Saturday night. On the Friday morning, David Ward, the leading bass-baritone of the company, who had spent many of his earlier years in a seminary, suggested he would sing the lovely plain-chant laments alternating with me. These chants were sad ones and were simply made for two bass-baritone voices, but it was to be the very last time I ever sang them. A decade later, we would have the emergence of the new Good Friday afternoon liturgy.

On the Saturday night at 11.30 p.m., about eight of the cast, including the Catholic musical director, came down to form the choir for the Midnight Mass. They glanced at Kitson's polyphonic Mass for ten minutes before the start of the Mass, after singing *Rigeletto* that Saturday night at the theatre. Only half of the group were Catholics and so most of them had never even seen the score before. I was acting as deacon at the Mass that night, and I can remember sitting with the celebrant and the sub-deacon at the side of the altar during the singing of the Gloria, vainly trying to 'choke back' the tears of joy and emotion as the Sadlers Wells Octet raised the roof with a sound that had all the power of a fifty-strong choir. If ever I was close to the joy of Heaven, it was that Saturday night in St Mary's!

Don't mistake me, liturgy today can be good; however, it needs a great deal of preparation and some talent, also. In the 1990s, lots of Catholics seek out good liturgy - the car makes this possible for them and given a choice, I always advise Catholics, especially converts, to find a church with a Sunday liturgy where they are comfortable. Of course, it would be even better if they used their talents to help provide a liturgy in their own parish that is good. However, much depends on us priests to enable them to achieve this.

CHAPTER XV

ROKER PARK

Roker Park holds many memories for me. Imagine a team playing in the Second Division, as it then was, for a great part of the 1950s, and yet drawing crowds of sixty thousand! Liverpool, Leeds and Newcastle all spent periods of exile in the lower division too. However, part of the great rivalry between Sunderland and Newcastle stemmed from the fact that they always had a potential one hundred and twenty thousand fans between them, even though St James's Park and Roker Park were only twelve miles apart.

Saturday football was 'out' for me because of the early start for Saturday confessions. However, my friendship with some of the Roker stars and with physiotherapist Johnny Watters, kept me in close touch with events at Roker. Midweek matches, cup matches and replays would see me making my way to the games and leaving my Francis Barnett motorbike - I had gone up a few ccs from my Darlington BSA Bantam days - in St Benet's church yard! St Benet's was within easy walking distance of Roker Park.

My own playing days continued throughout my Sunderland years, but I had to be content with Wednesday League football now that Saturdays were out of the question for me. After starting with the Ryhope & District Wednesday League team, the Sunderland GPO, I soon joined a great group of lads from various walks in life. Captain, Don Maxwell, owned a flourishing DIY shop in Sunderland. Our team boasted a plumber, an electrician, a heating engineering firm boss and various other types. I suppose it was equally strange for them to have a Catholic priest as their goalkeeper! We called ourselves 'Sunderland Amateurs' and for several years we were one of the outstanding midweek teams in the area. There was a great spirit among the players and because we always played for each other, we proved very hard to beat. At first, the lads were a bit shy with me. This was never so evident as when we had the luxury of showers or bathing facilities after one of our away wins and spirits were high. We had a great character called Lex Barker who played centre forward. Lex's vocabulary was naturally fairly fruity at the best of times. Don Maxwell would often gently quieten Lex down a bit with the words 'remember the Father'. In deference to me, swearing was usually reserved for outside the dressing room, and must have demanded considerable restraint on the part of some of my team mates.

I suppose my exploits in the local Wednesday League led to strengthening the bonds I had already made with some of the Roker players. Charlie Hurley, who recently was deservedly voted 'Roker Player of the Century' became a very close friend. Soon after his arrival at Sunderland from Millwall, he brought his fiancée, Joan, to me to take instruction in the Catholic Faith. After their subsequent marriage, we remained lifelong friends. Sadly, though, we have not seen too much of each other since Charlie moved south when his playing days were over. I remember introducing him and Jim McNab to tennis during the days when Charlie was the 'King of Roker'. Later on, after his football days were over, Charlie and Joan, his wife, were to become very keen tennis players. We kept promising on Christmas cards that we would get together again on the tennis court, but unfortunately never managed it with a 300-mile gap between us. However the Rhys Evans family helped me always to fill any tennis gap. Jean, Rhys and the children had a private court, and between Rhys's ENT operating sessions we pursued a great tennis rivalry.

Brian Clough, another Roker favourite, joined us on one or two occasions at Thorn Hill Tennis Club. Brian was just as competitive on the tennis court as he was on the football field. Unlike Charlie and Jim, 'Cloughie' was already a very competent tennis player! On court, he displayed the same self-confidence and anticipation that made him such a deadly goal scorer. What a tragedy that his brilliant playing career was cut short. In a game near Christmas against Norwich, he sportingly tried to avoid a collision with the Norwich goalkeeper chasing a 50/50 ball, and tore his cruciate ligaments. Clough was the most instinctive goal-scoring machine I ever saw before he became one of the all-time great managers. However, except for his tragic injury, he could have become one of the greatest goal-scorers of all time! Before he came to Sunderland he had scored over forty goals a season with Middlesbrough for several seasons. His short record with Sunderland was fifty-four goals in sixty-one games.

Another Roker friend I could not miss out is Billy Elliott. Both as a player and later as a manager of Sunderland, Bill and I never lost touch. His wife Peggy, a Yorkshire lass who could get quite carried away during a match, would often take me to Roker Park to sit next to her in the main stand. Poor Peggy, who was a devout Catholic, would frequently have to apologize to her priest-companion after displaying a certain lack of charity and forbearance to some unfortunate referee. Referees did not always see 'incidents' involving Billy in the same light as we did, and to complicate matters even further, everybody knows that Billy was a very wholehearted player.

However, possibly the greatest Roker Park thrill of the 1950s, was the 'Roker Roar' that would start up when 'King Charlie', as Hurley was known, would start his famous casual, loping run upfield for a corner kick or a set piece. Charlie was undoubtedly the first of the attacking centre-backs. His powerful timing in the air and his tremendous strength, created panic in opposing defences. He could usually threaten a goal with a direct header, or indirectly, by his great ability to lay the ball off with his head for one of his lurking forwards. Nowadays, the 'Big Men at the Back' automatically move up for corners and set pieces, but the game is completely different. Numbers on shirts merely identify players - in the 1950s, they identified positions. Arguably, only the Mannions and Carters of yesteryear would have been completely comfortable with the 1990s game.

THE ROSARY CRUSADE

One of the memories of Roker Park - sadly now itself defunct - I feel I should share with you is one that was in direct connection with my *priesthood.*

An American priest called Father Patrick Peyton had been drawing huge crowds in the USA, organizing prayer rallies, just as a Protestant evangelist, Billy Graham, had been drawing crowds in the same way. Like Bishop Fulton Sheen, Peyton had also attracted a huge television audience. Fulton Sheen's telecasts had attracted millions who were enthralled by his direct and simple method of communicating the Gospel Message, with nothing more than a blackboard and chalk as stage props.

Father Peyton was probably not the theological communicator that Fulton Sheen was, but his simple holiness and sincerity impressed audiences in the 1950s, rather like the legendary Mother Teresa has impressed millions in the 1980s and 1990s. Peyton's message was simple: 'The family that prays together, stays together.' 'Prayers' for Peyton was 'The Rosary', and his rallies became known as Rosary Crusades.

He was coming to England and one of the venues was to be the north-east. The management of Sunderland Football Club offered Roker Park for the rally, after some hesitation from St James's Park, Newcastle. A small committee of local priests was commissioned to assist Father Murphy (Father Peyton's organizing lieutenant) in whatever way he directed.

Father Dan deputed me to 'carry the flag' from St Mary's. I was especially to work on the publicity side with the *Sunderland Echo.* The *Echo* had assigned one of their young reporters, Joe Cummings, who was its reporter for the theatre! Joe was a fine young Catholic and he often contacted me about stories of people who were appearing at the Sunderland Empire, if I had already met them during my Catholic Stage Guild work.

On one occasion we welcomed to the Empire together, a young man who was making his big-time Debut there - Tommy Steele went on to become a huge star and still is today. Sadly Joe died prematurely some years ago. However, Pat, his widow, still cherishes a wonderful letter which he received from Tommy thanking him for his 'encouragement' when his foot was on that very first rung of the Ladder of Fame!

Joe liaised with me about the best way to make the Rally a success. He was an enthusiastic and well-informed writer, but later acquired national fame as a sports writer and TV commentator. His deep Catholic faith enabled him to understand perfectly what a Rosary Crusade was about; between us we mounted a very successful publicity campaign.

Through the Sisters of Mercy and their wonderful contacts in all the schools and parishes, we were able to follow up the plentiful and extensive *Echo* publicity. One of the memorable methods we used was to organize a 'Living Rosary' made up of girls from St Anthony's Grammar School in their uniforms, spread around the whole of the Roker Park football pitch in the exact shape of a Rosary. The Cross of the Rosary would actually become part of the huge podium, from which Father Peyton addressed the crowd. The spectacle from the highest point of the main stand was simply breathtaking – the whole thirty thousand crowd thronging the ground must have felt wonderfully proud of their Faith. For many years afterwards, it was always refreshing for a priest to meet families who had adopted the slogan of Father Peyton in their daily family lives: 'The family that prays together, stays together.' So long as family prayer endured, it was to be a wonderful blessing. In the second half of my priestly life, however, daily family prayer more or less disappeared, especially when it had to compete against television.

CHAPTER XVI

SHADES OF DAMON RUNYON

P.G. Wodehouse was very popular reading in my Seminary days, just as Damon Runyon was 'accepted' reading by the forward-looking priests of the 1950s. My fellow curate, Father Leo and myself held the author of *Guys and Dolls* and *The Lemon Drop Kid* in the highest regard. Indeed, we had a secret agreement that half of Runyon's characters were alive and well in that part of Sunderland called St Mary's Parish. The police, the bookmakers, the taxi drivers, the Likely Lads of the city centre, and the 'Hard boys' who made the occasional dodgy quid, they all lived within a couple of hundred yards of St Mary's Church; and most of them even retained an on-off allegiance with it. Harry the Horse, Big Lukie, Louis the Lug, Regret the Horse Player, Ropes McGonigle - all of them found reincarnation in half a dozen characters who haunted Mackey's Corner, the betting shop or the Station End. Many a short story from Runyon we saw re-enacted time after time on our own doorstep!

One of our favourite stories was the one where one of Runyon's newly reformed and successful characters has 'made it good', and has become very respectable. This character has a great devotion to his old mother and when she dies, he is obsessed with the notion that she will have the greatest funeral ever seen on Broadway. He spends thousands of dollars on flowers and limousines and packing the church. One of our great characters in St Mary's, by that time a very influential bookmaker, was John Wharton. John had become very successful, and *respectable* with it. He was the leader, or boss man, of quite a large 'clan'. He epitomized the bookie who really had it made. His expensive Crombie overcoat, his shining shoes and his heavily-ringed fingers all pointed to a newly acquired opulence. He would lead the 'clan', sometimes twenty of them, into the corner chapel in St Mary's Church most Sundays for the 9.30 a.m. Mass, especially after a successful day at Doncaster on the Saturday! At the end of the Mass, John would peel off several fivers from the wad of notes he flourished and ask Father Dan to 'keep the Masses going'. Sometimes, however, after a hard Saturday night, John would not appear at the 9.30 a.m. Sunday Mass and the 'Wharton private chapel' would be empty. Innocently, one day I reminded him that there was always the eleven o'clock Mass if they were too late for the 9.30 a.m. John was absolutely horrified at the suggestion, saying, 'No Wharton ever goes to the eleven o'clock Mass, Father. That's for the "by-the-way" Catholics.'

Now John, like many a head of a dynasty, had a reverential devotion to his mother - the 'old lady', as he respectfully called her. Many of the clan lived in East Cross Street down by the river, one of several streets that have long disappeared. One Monday, when I was 'on duty', I had been called to see 'the old lady' who had been taken ill. John thought it only right that I should continue and minister to her with Holy Communion and the Blessing of the Sick whenever this was necessary in future. Since she was beginning to 'fail', I got to know John fairly well. He had been a professional boxer, among other things, and we often had quite spirited arguments about the professional boxing scene.

Inevitably, the day came when my blessing didn't save her and John summoned me. He told me that he wanted to give 'the old lady' a very special send-off: nothing would be spared. He wanted 'The Boss' (Father Dan) to say the Mass, but I was to be the MC for the proceedings. John, himself, would see to the police about the traffic, because there would be several cars! St Mary's was on the main street of the city and had steps going straight down from the church door into the busiest street in Sunderland - Bridge Street/Fawcett Street. There would be a lot of people in the church, and St Mary's was a huge square church, with a very large choir gallery. It was possible to pack a thousand people into that church - something we did regularly every Sunday night in the 1950s, once we had started a Sunday evening Mass!

On the day of the funeral Mass, there was traffic chaos outside the church. Trams were lined up halfway down Fawcett Street, waiting for the cortège to move. John knew only too well that many of the 'invited' mourners would need a later Mass that day to ensure that they arrived. St Mary's was heaving! Apart from the seven hundred seated, there must have been another three or four hundred standing wherever they could get in. Scores of mourners who had never darkened the church for years, apart from the occasional St Patrick's Day Mass, were there resplendent in their funeral finery. My friend, Father Peter Starrs, who was doing some house calls later that morning, was proudly told by the wife of Big Lukie, that Lukie was at Mass as though it was the most natural place in the world to look for Big Lukie when he wasn't at home!

STAGE GUILD CHAPLAINCY

My ministry as Chaplain to the Catholic Stage Guild in Sunderland provided so many interesting memories that I could write a book on that ministry alone. To anybody who was contemporary with the provincial theatre scene of the 1950s, my present abbreviated account may seem a trifle self-indulgent, or even an exercise in name-dropping. But surely that was in the very nature of the whole apostolate. Georgie Wood had persuaded the Cardinal that this apostolate was important. I have already told you that all variety performers, whether they were top of the bill stars or complete unknowns in the chorus line, were constantly travelling from one theatre to the next. They could actually be living out of a suitcase for almost fifty-two weeks of the year if they were successful with continuous work. They were rarely at home. If they were to talk to a priest at all, it had to be on their travels, hence the setting up of the Catholic Stage Guild.

Although undoubtedly I found it interesting to meet many of the people who had become famous, or who would later become famous, in the years that followed, nevertheless, I approached this work very much as a routine part of my Sunderland priesthood. In eight years I hardly ever missed a week when I did not call backstage to look after the welfare of all the artists who were visiting the Empire that week. Some of them were household names, but most of them were comparatively unknown. Confessions, return to the Sacraments, convert instruction, convalidation of marriage . . . all of these routine pastoral duties became a normal part of a very fruitful Catholic Stage Guild ministry. However, there was one major handicap: like all English priests prior to 1965, I was forbidden by an archaic law from actually attending a theatrical performance. In all my eight years' work as theatre chaplain, I never saw a show at Sunderland Empire from the auditorium! However, my weekly contact provided many opportunities to 'help'. This help, in turn, often provoked a response from the performers themselves. Such a response would often be triggered off by a genuine gratitude that 'The Church' was interested in their art and their welfare. It would sow the seeds of friendships, some of which would last a lifetime. Others there would be that might last for many years before death finally intervened. Some of my friends of forty-plus years, like Val Doonican, Frankie Vaughan, Guy Mitchell and others, are still very much around and despite distance we still mutually cherish our friendship. Others like Winifred Atwell, and Ruby Murray, both very dear friends, have passed on back to the Good Lord. I have interesting memories of all of them, which I should share with you as their possible fans and admirers.

I have poignant memories of others, too, whom I met, like Laurel and Hardy, who never became friends in the accepted sense, but who made a lasting impression on me! Maybe I could pen a memoir or two of each of them in the following pages.

CHAPTER XVII

CITY HALL IMPRESARIO

Val Doonican, I will take first, since the foreword to this book makes Val the person who actually persuaded me to write these memoirs. We all need to be pushed a little in life. Most of us tend to be easy-going in our leisure time, especially if we are workaholics in our 'day job'. Val himself had been pushed into doing his autobiographical *Walking Tall* and *The Special Years* by 1950s actor David Niven. Niven, after listening fascinated to Val's story-telling during dinner one night, had bluntly said to Val, 'You realize, Val, that all these stories will die with you if you don't write them down and share them with others.' Niven had just completed his own autobiography with his best-selling *The Moon's a Balloon.*

Val, as I have mentioned already, was a leading member of a vocal group of the early 1950s called The Four Ramblers. He was unmarried at the time and was the 'bread ticket' for the others in the group. He was the musician and was responsible for the musical arrangements, the band parts and the band calls. He stayed on with his friends a long time because they were really dependent on his talents to keep them working, so perhaps this is why it took him almost twenty years to become an 'overnight success'. The talent that Val so clearly displays now in a two-hour, one-man show, celebrating fifty years in showbusiness, was already latent in the early 1950s. Even at that time he could completely fascinate a crowd of his peers at any party with a rich tapestry of songs, humour and wonderful stories. The polish, the wit and the technique have all developed, of course, as a result of his pioneering of TV live shows during twenty-five years of TV shows at peak viewing times. But the talent, the latent talent, was always there.

Stories about Val? So numerous, but just let us remember one or two. You remember my illustrious parish priest, Father Dan

O'Donovan? Father Dan was a Cork man and he was inclined to take himself very seriously. Talking to Val one day outside St Mary's, he had been a teeny-weeny bit dismissive about Val's Waterford origins. Val had then asked Father Dan where he came from, having a good idea from his accent that it was Cork. Father Dan had told him with some pride, 'Conakilty, County Cork.'

With an irreverent twinkle in his eye, Val had quickly said to Father Dan, 'You know what we say in Waterford, Father? The best thing that ever came out of Cork was the road to Waterford.' Father Dan was not amused . . .

Later on that night he suddenly turned on me at supper with, 'God Jack, that friend of yours, Doonican, is an impudent fellow!'

Perhaps Father Dan forgave him when, years later, he would recognize Val who would be hosting his television series on Father Dan's dining room TV, by that time, a very famous personality. I remember he did tell me how he enjoyed *The Val Doonican Show.*

I learned from my friendship with Val and other famous personalities like Frankie Vaughan, that one never presumed on their friendship to elicit favours. I have forfeited the friendship of one or two people, including priests, in my lifetime, when I have refused to implicate my famous friends in fund-raising events, however worthy the cause! In June 1964 the church at Dipton where I was a curate was burned down by a pyromaniac who was later admitted to St Nicholas's Psychiatric Hospital in Newcastle. The complete story I will tell later. The church insurance was grossly inadequate as with most churches at that time, and the story received national coverage. Val, who by this time was becoming famous with his early TV series, contacted me and offered his services. If I could book a venue, he would put a show together and do a concert for the church building fund. I immediately became 'impresario'. Thinking as big as possible, I booked the City Hall, Newcastle. Obviously, all the publicity had to be undertaken privately and not on a commercial basis. I readily persuaded many of my Irish priest friends to organize coaches and parties for the night. Val, who had just completed his first BBC Saturday Night TV series, invited one or two of his guests from the series to join him. There was a young comedian, described on the programme as one of the great up-and-coming comedians - 'You will love him.' His name just happened to be Les Dawson - how prophetic that description was to be! Then there was a delightful musical duo called The Dalmours (David and Marianne Dalmour). Their love-song chemistry was almost palpable. They later became wonderful friends of mine, but a few years later they mutually agreed to retire from the business and have been living quietly near Leeds Airport for many years. Denny Piercy, one of the best compères in showbusiness at the time, compèred the whole show and a local music group called The Silver Dollars completed the entertainment. The show was a delightful one and was a complete sell-out. Val's generosity and that of his artiste friends gave us a tremendous boost with the Restoration Fund. Today, a beautiful modern church has replaced the former smaller St Patrick's Church, which was so gutted by the fire it had to be completely demolished.

CHAPTER XVIII

YOUTH CLUBS AND NANNIES

Frankie Vaughan I met when he was an up-and-coming singer, but not yet famous. A Jewish friend of his from Sunderland, a fine impersonator called Eddie Arnold, introduced us. Eddie's promising career was tragically cut short when he died from a brain tumour while still a young man and at an important stage in his career. His charming wife, Mary, was left to bring up their little daughter, Debbie, who later became a well-known personality and actress in *The Two Ronnies* and other shows!

Returning one Monday morning on my motorbike from the early morning Convent Mass, I recognized a familiar figure in the High Street, Sunderland. Frank had been unable to get a taxi in the taxi rank, and had decided to step out the two hundred or so yards from the station to the theatre. I did a U-turn on my motorbike and soon had him on the pillion, with his case wedged between us - he was absolutely shattered after his all-night travels. I decided to take him immediately to one of our 'star' stage digs which was run by Mrs Phillips in Riversdale Terrace. Later he made this his home on all his future visits to Sunderland . . . as indeed did many stars. Some of them preferred to stay in comfortable homely 'digs' rather than in the more formal Grand Hotel.

Frank and I had one absorbing thing in common - youth clubs! I was already running this huge, mixed club at St Mary's, and Frank was just beginning his legendary work for boys' clubs. We became firm friends from the very beginning. His later visits to Sunderland Empire were to follow his huge hits like 'Green Door', 'Give me the Moonlight' and many others. By that time, when he visited as top-of-the-bill, the Empire would be sold out weeks before. Stella, Frank's lovely wife, liked to tour with him when it was at all possible. When their two children were at the toddling stage, Stella approached me to see if I could find a reliable nanny in my youth club, who would be prepared to go and live with them in London as one of the family. I found just the girl – Liz Traynor was one of a large family of children. At nineteen she was a no-nonsense young lady who did the books for me for the Parish Football Pool. She was a girl who got on with her work without the constant 'encouragement' often required by some of her peers. She went to the Vaughan home in London on 17 November 1957 and settled in as to the manor born! Indeed, she soon became a very integral part of the household and remained so for the next six years. When Frank and Stella went to Hollywood to make his famous film with Marilyn Monroe, she went with them, and because of the first ever Equity strike, they had to remain in Hollywood for six months! Frank was insistent that I should always visit them for the night whenever I was passing through London. He wanted me to feel sure that she was being afforded the opportunity to practise her Faith and was actually practising it.

Another thing that Frank and I had in common was fishing. I remember vividly one time when I was on holiday in Worthing with my mother, and Frank was appearing at the Brighton Empire in a summer season. He had some good friends down in Newhaven and they would line up some excellent bass fishing from the Newhaven pier. One night he invited me to accompany him. In order to facilitate a speedy exit from the theatre at 10.30 p.m. he asked me if I could bring my old 'jalopy' to the back of the theatre, and he would make his escape – there would be no autographs on that particular night! As we trundled away there were curious looks from people in the streets, almost saying, 'Doesn't he look like Frankie Vaughan . . . but it couldn't be in a car like that!' When we arrived at Newhaven pier Frank's fishermen friends already had the lines baited. It was a mild, balmy night and the hours just slipped away – Frank and his friends were very successful and between them they landed several beautiful sea bass – six- or seven-pounders! I was not so lucky. Towards the end of the session, however, I struggled with what must have been a 'beauty', but in my inexperience, I lost it. I dropped off Frank at the lovely country house that they were renting for the summer season, with a handsome bass for Stella to cook. When I eventually stole quietly into my mother's house near Worthing, the sun was just beginning to glimmer on the eastern horizon.

The sequel: shortly after this, I became parish priest in Sedgefield - the first time I was to get my feet under my own table as a priest. The following Christmas, and every Christmas for the first ten years I was there, amongst my spate of Christmas greetings would arrive a neat A4-size large plastic envelope with the name 'Goodfare' on it. Yes, you've guessed - it was a hefty pack of smoked salmon, with the cryptic message 'This is for the one that got away, Love, Frank and Stella.'

Postscript about Liz Traynor: she was eventually to leave the Vaughan family and after a short spell with the British Ambassador in Kuwait, she married Robin Green, a naval commander, and one of the Falkland War heroes. To this day we often have a good laugh when I insist that in those early years in London, she subconsciously 'deserted' her Sunderland accent for what, in the 1960s, we would have described as an 'Oxford Accent'! Needless to say, she still tells me, 'I think you are just imagining this, Oncle Jaques.'

CHAPTER XIX

THE BLACK TUXEDO (Guy Mitchell)

One of the most popular singing stars to play The Empire in the 1950s, along with Johnny Ray, Al Martino, Ted Hockridge, David Whitfield, Tommy Steel and a score of others, was Guy Mitchell.

Guy already had a string of international hits to his credit at the time. He had an infectious voice that churned out No. 1s with almost boring predictability. His hit songs were an amalgam of pop and country-western, tinged with a large dash of humour and escapism!

Guy's family were originally Croat, and his mother was a devout Croat Catholic. Mindful of his mother's aspirations for him, Guy made contact with me early in his week at The Empire. He was staying, literally, across the road from St Mary's in the Grand Hotel. As soon as he saw St Mary's Church from his hotel room window he decided that this was the answer to his mother's prayers, and he duly made his Easter Confession and Communion. We became instant friends and remained friends for the next forty years. Guy had a great zest for life and his generous spirit had to be constantly disciplined. I finally persuaded him that I did not need a 'bigger and better motorbike'. Nevertheless, he threatened me that he 'would *think* of something . . .'

A couple of years later he finished a season at the London Palladium, when he had a huge hit, 'Singing the Blues', and entered the London Clinic for a knee operation. I was visiting my mother for my summer holiday - by this time she had moved to Goring-by-Sea, near Worthing, after my father's death. I had come up to town by train, intending to stay the night with Val Doonican and his mother. Guy was convalescing in the Savoy Hotel so I had arranged to go and have lunch with him and spend a few hours there. Val was to come up by car to the Savoy about 6 p.m. to collect me. During the extended room-service lunch,

Guy's former 'Miss World' wife joined us in the suite. She was halfway through a shopping spree and informed Guy that she had saved him 'a thousand dollars' with a couple of her purchases. She decided to model one of the dresses for his approval and, giving me a wink on the blind side of Guy, she said naively, 'How do you like it, Father?' in an engaging Swedish accent. I responded to her prompting by assuring Guy and her that it was 'out of this world'. I was thinking to myself that if you clothed this lady in an old sack with some strategic holes in it, she would still look 'out of this world'. Mission accomplished, she then reminded Guy that he intended to have me try on his black tuxedo which he had worn a few days earlier at the Palladium. Guy produced it and had me try it on. She was quite positive - it fitted me better than it fitted him! In due course the room-service bell was again pressed and the tuxedo was dispatched to the Savoy in-house tailor to be dry-cleaned and pressed immediately for its future priestly use!

Now, in the 1990s, occasionally I have to dress up for a special dinner, cocktail party or wedding reception. Friends and fellow guests often remark on the black mohair tuxedo. It has been beautifully relined on two occasions by expert needlewomen of my parish. On the first occasion, by Tess Malloy, who died many years ago, and latterly, by Dorothy Williamson, who is fortunately still with us. I am still the twelve and a half stones that I was when Guy gave it to me, so it still fits me perfectly. In my earlier years, when people commented on it, I would say to them, 'Guy Mitchell wore this on his last appearance at the London Palladium.'

Even then, I could see some of them giving me a quizzical look, and holding back the repartee, 'You're joking, of course, Father.'

Nowadays, in the 1990s, I don't say anything - especially if those paying me the compliment are under forty! The star names of the 1950s mean nothing whatsoever to them; indeed, they may not even be known to them! These people belong to a generation that never even saw the Beatles on TV, let alone in concert!

When Val arrived at the Savoy to collect me, he was brought up to Guy's room. By this time Guy was in high spirits. He had a crutch to help him get about and he was doing his impersonation of Long John Silver. Guy was at heart a frustrated actor, even though he had actually appeared in one or two lesser-known films. Occasionally he would disappear on his crutch to the 'pantry' that adjoins all the exclusive suites of the Savoy, to regale himself with a Bloody Mary. Val was still with The Four Ramblers at the time and had never worked with Guy, but he was soon 'sucked in' to the party. Guy had been strumming a guitar that was lying on the sofa and singing with gusto. I introduced Val to him and told him Val was a musician with a vocal group. Guy's opening remark to Val was, 'Do you play guitar?'

Val replied, 'Yes, a little.'

Guy immediately passed him the guitar to keep the party going. Val obliged and played a beautiful, intricate, instrumental piece. I was watching Guy's face as Val's fingers deftly moved up and down the neck of the guitar and I could see the look of amazement and incredulity as he suddenly went uncannily quiet! As Val finished, Guy leant over to him and said with a simple, unbelievable candour, 'Hey bud, how come I never heard of you?'

Many years later, Guy would remember that Savoy evening, when Val had become a huge star with the same bill-topping fame that Guy himself had enjoyed in the 1950s. It was very late that night when Val and I extricated ourselves with difficulty from the Savoy! Guy was enjoying the impromptu party and sing-song that ensued, so much so, that he was loath to let us go.

CHAPTER XX

WISE CHILD - *MY FIRST VISIT TO THE THEATRE - WINIFRED ATWELL*

On one of my journeys to see my mother near Worthing, I had arranged to break off in London and have lunch with Winifred Atwell. Winnie was one of the outstanding acts of the late 1950s. She was a Jamaican-born pharmacist, who was also a very accomplished pianist - her musical talent rather submerged her pharmaceutical talent, and so she became a concert pianist in England. She also had the idea of using an old, battered 'honky-tonk' piano as part of her musical act. On her honky-tonk piano, she would play a completely contrasting rhythmic, jazz-style music which required great dexterity and speed of finger. This alternative playing became hugely popular and she had several No. 1 hits in quick succession, such as 'Black & White Rag'.

She was already top-of-the-bill when she first visited Sunderland Empire. Winnie was very happy to have the opportunity to talk seriously to a priest and we became very firm friends. She came to Mass at St Mary's with great joy on several occasions. On one of these occasions, after the eleven o'clock Sunday High Mass, we found a large, crisp, white £5 note - the old type - in the midst of the pennies and shillings and occasional half-crowns in the collection box. I mentioned casually to the incredulous Father Dan, who was sitting in his armchair while the curates counted the collection, that it was probably Winifred Atwell from The Empire who had contributed the fiver - the first fiver I had ever seen in a St Mary's collection. Father Dan obviously rejoiced that the Catholic Stage Guild Apostolate was bearing fruit in more ways than one as he piped up from the chair, 'God, Jack, how long is she staying?'

As I stated earlier, Winnie was to entertain me to lunch at her mews flat after breaking my journey to Worthing. She was a fabulous cook when she had the time to be one. After lunch Winnie said she knew that now, after the Vatican Council, I was 'officially' allowed to go to the theatre. She had tried to book for a matinee of *My Fair Lady*, but it was sold out. Instead, she had booked seats for the latest Alec Guinness play, *Wise Child* at Wyndham's Theatre. She told me she did not know much about the play, but 'it had to be good if Guinness was in it.' I was so excited in my anticipation. I had loved Guinness in *Kind Hearts & Coronets* and other Ealing comedies, and I couldn't wait to make my first visit to a famous West End theatre!

With time to spare, we went out to get a cab for Wyndham's, but to our utter dismay, it proved impossible. It was the first day after the Drink and Drive breathalyser law and it seemed that half of London was avoiding driving that day - every cab within a half-mile radius appeared to have been taken. In sheer desperation, as the performance time drew near, Lou Levison, Winnie's husband, had to get out the Rolls.

We finally arrived at the theatre five minutes late. Winnie had booked a box for us and after some confusion, we were ushered in.

The Author with Winifred Atwell, 1954-5

The Assistant Manager was a keen fan of Winnie's and she had to restrain him when we found our box had already been occupied. After a certain amount of commotion, Winnie insisted on our going into the empty box on the opposite side of the stage. At that time, at Wyndhams, the boxes were almost part of the stage itself. Strictly, we should have waited for the interval, but Winnie's manager fan insisted that we must slip in immediately. We went into the box as quietly as possible but a sea of faces in the auditorium focused immediately on our box to see who was arriving, and Winnie was immediately recognised - I could hear the whispers. I had on my black suit and a very visible plastic clerical collar - the wide, full-frontal type popular at that time. My dog-collar must have gleamed out in the stage lighting.

We had no idea about the plot - it seemed that Guinness was masquerading as a woman after escaping from prison with a teenage boy. Most of the action took place in a rather sleazy, small hotel where the owner was a homosexual. The other main character was a scantily-clad black chambermaid who was very conspicuous on stage. The young boy with Guinness became a target for the homosexual hotel owner. In the early 1960s West End scripts were beginning to show a rather risqué flavour and *Wise Child* was no exception - there were frequent references to 'queers' and 'niggers', depending on whether the hotel manager or the coloured chambermaid was actually being referred to on stage. The plot was thin and entirely predictable, so most of the matinee audience were more interested in seeing how Winnie and her priest companion in the box were reacting. Any reference to 'niggers' and the sea of faces beyond the stage would turn upwards to see how Winnie had taken it. Any reference to 'queers' or any swearing - and there was quite a lot of that - and the sea of faces would again swing upwards to see how the wearer of the shiny clerical collar was taking it. I tried to press myself back in the box, sweating profusely with embarrassment! Winnie kept apologizing to me and suggested we should leave, but I thought we would become even more conspicuous by leaving than by staying. Eventually, after one of the most embarrassing hours in my life, the interval arrived and we gratefully slipped away. I had waited forty years to see my first professional stage performance and it was a disaster! Poor Winnie was so embarrassed for me - she never stopped apologizing until I left later that evening to catch the Brighton express. I suspect *Wise Child* must have been taken off after only a few weeks as I never saw it advertised again. It must have been the only failure Alec Guinness ever had in his long and illustrious career!

Winnie's worldwide popularity was to prove very costly. She went out to do a three-month season in Australia which proved so popular that she stayed on for fifteen months! During that time one of her UK accountants embezzled thousands of pounds which she sent home. Moreover, she was absent from the British circuit here so long that a good-looking young man called Russ Conway, who also played a honky-tonk piano in his act, quickly filled the gap that she had left. After a brief return to this country, Winnie went out again to Australia, a country that she had come to love. She settled down there until her premature death which I only heard about some weeks later.

I often gaze at a beautiful golden cross embedded in some solid plastic colourless base, which Winnie brought me from Hawaii, and which adorns my mantlepiece in Sedgefield. It reminds me vividly of a cultured and warm friend who so wanted to make my first visit to the theatre a memorable one. If only Winnie had known what *Wise Child* was about before she booked . . . if only *My Fair Lady* had not been sold out.

CHAPTER XXI

LESSONS IN HUMILITY

No. 1 - RUBY MURRAY

I have often had to preach on the topic of pride and its elusive contrary virtue, humility. In my Theatre Apostolate I met examples of both - at various times I met people who found it difficult to cope with success and stardom, whereas I met others who were never fazed by it at all.

Ruby Murray is a name which immediately springs to my mind. Ruby came to The Empire in 1954 as a nineteen-year-old. She was on the verge of fame but not yet topping bills. She was appearing on a popular TV show at the time, *Quite Contrary.* Her nervous simplicity was part of her appeal on stage, but the truth was that Ruby was exactly the same off-stage. Val Doonican, who had just worked with her in Birmingham, telephoned me before her arrival in Sunderland. He asked me to look after her and 'fix her up' with Mrs Phillips - one of the nicest of stage-digs landladies - and Ruby duly arrived with Marie Cunningham, her pianist and road manager. Ruby was a Belfast Protestant and Marie was a Belfast Catholic! In those days, long before the Northern Ireland troubles had really escalated, they were as close as sisters. Ruby was impressed with my 'looking after' her, and we became lifelong friends after that first week in Sunderland. Within months, she was topping bills throughout the country and turning out No. 1 hits; in the next few hectic years, she was to achieve worldwide fame. She was to do something that even the Beatles never managed to achieve - she had five hits in the Top 20 all at the same time! Only Elvis Presley, and later Madonna, were ever to equal this record. Her greatest hit, 'Softly, Softly', was to remain in the charts for nearly a year!

The trouble, however, with Ruby at the height of her fame, was that she couldn't really believe it was actually happening. She was too humble and simple in her outlook to cope with the demands of her stardom. Even at the height of this fame, Ruby's philosophy was 'anything for a simple life'. She found it difficult to be in any way confrontational and yet, so often in life, we have to take a stand and occasionally make difficult decisions. Problems don't disappear as a result of our procrastination - they usually get worse!

When the provincial theatre took a bit of a hammering in the middle 1960s, we saw the emergence of the large clubs as entertainment venues. Some of the old theatres either disappeared or were taken over by local authorities so that these large clubs became the only places that could pay the salaries of the bigger stars. With their huge profit from drinks, and later food, they were the only venues that could

The Author with Ruby Murray

afford their visits. The result was that many variety theatre circuit performers had to change their acts quite drastically. This applied especially to singers, who had to develop a smooth cabaret-style act, lasting maybe sixty minutes, instead of performing a compact medley of their own hit songs and other popular songs, which might have lasted only forty-five minutes. Poor Ruby found the transition fraught with trauma when she discovered that with the help of an early brandy she could actually become quite a talented comedienne for the night, as well as a popular singer. The cost of this transition was to affect both her happiness and eventually her health itself.

For forty years and more, I would always receive a Christmas note from her signed 'Your Wee Orange-Woman'. Ruby always retained her Protestant faith, despite her mother's initial worries that she might convert to Catholicism. Her mother once warned me that it would embarrass her father, Dan, who was a staunch member of a Belfast Orange Lodge, if she ever converted. Sadly, during her last twenty years of life, our meetings became more infrequent. She rarely worked in the North, and our contact depended on occasional phone calls or letters.

Christmas of 1995 passed and, for the first time in forty years I received no greeting from Ruby. I thought perhaps she had the flu or something and had not been able to send Christmas greetings, however, in early September 1996, I received a rather sad notelet. The heading on the note was 'Asprey's Nursing Home, Torquay'. It read:

> Dear Father John, the reason I haven't been in touch with you is I have been in and out of hospital for about eighteen months (nearly shook hands with The Big Fella twice . . . but he must have decided it wasn't time yet.) I'm happy to say I'm well on the way back – but maybe you'd say a prayer for me – I have faith, you know!
>
> Here's me going on about myself . . . how are you, dear friend? Well, I hope! Give all my love to Vera and all my friends up there, etc. etc.

Thank God, I didn't wait to write. I immediately discovered the telephone number of the nursing home from directory enquiries, and that same day telephoned Ruby; we had a wonderful chat for nearly half an hour.

A couple of weeks later I received another notelet. Ruby was saying, 'I think about you often. Please keep praying for me. Lots of love, Ruby.' Again, I telephoned and again we had a long conversation. Unfortunately, I thought that she was actually getting better as I thought the prognosis was good. In fact, although she did not know it at the time, her illness was terminal. I asked her to get her son, Timmy, to put her on the train to come North for some convalescence, but obviously, she was not fit enough to do this. When someone telephoned me on 17 December to say that it had been on the news that Ruby Murray had died, I was shattered. I told her son, Tim, on the telephone that unfortunately, because of my many duties here in the parish at Christmas time, I would not be able to attend her funeral. However, I was able to trace her old friend, Marie Cunningham, through the *Daily Mail* article about Ruby, and after a lapse of thirty-five years, Marie and I discussed old times as she filled me in with the detail about Ruby's final years.

No. 2 - LAUREL AND HARDY

My second lesson in humility, and undoubtedly the most memorable lesson of my whole life, was my meeting with Laurel and Hardy. In 1952, they undertook a farewell tour of Great Britain which was to include only five venues. At that time, they were huge stars - legends in their own lifetime! Stan Laurel had spent some of his childhood in Bishop Auckland and so it was decided that the Sunderland Empire would be one of the five theatres they would play. Even for the biggest stars in the world, playing the Sunderland Empire in 1952 meant at least four and a half hours each night confined to the building. They would be on-stage for approximately one and three-quarter hours of that time - the rest of the time they would be in their dressing rooms.

Consequently, when a rather nervous young priest knocked at the door of the No. 1 dressing room and said, 'I'm Father Caden, the priest from the Catholic Stage Guild,' the door was opened by Stan

Laurel with a welcoming smile, and I was graciously ushered in to their holy-of-holies!

He led me over to the other side of the dressing room where Oliver Hardy was relaxing with a book. He was seated at the performers' black worktop, with its large mirror 'haloed' with a dozen bright bulbs. He hauled himself out of his chair and with a wonderful 'Olly' smile, shook my hand and drawled, 'It's a pleasure to meet you, Father. Would you care for a drink?'

I declined, with a stammered, 'No thank you, all the same.'

'Please do take a seat, Father,' Olly insisted. If I had been the Pope, I couldn't have been made to feel more welcome! They talked to me about England, about my work as a priest and why I chose it, about the influence of the Catholic Church and the Episcopalian Church

Caricature - Laurel & Hardy

in America, and many other topics. As I sat there, I had to pinch myself to be sure that these were really the men who had enriched my schoolboy years and early manhood with so much laughter and pathos. They never once alluded to their film fame during our forty minutes conversation. When I tried to say how much happiness they had given me and millions more, Olly, with a deprecating smile, merely said, 'Thank you, Father, that's very gracious of you . . .' and gently changed the subject!

As a priest, I had often been intrigued with the personification of 'Wisdom' in the Old Testament Book of Wisdom - since 1952, I have never ceased to marvel at 'Humility' personified in the very disparate persons of Stan Laurel and Oliver Hardy.

Reluctantly, I must tear myself away from my Empire reminiscences. I have touched on just a few highlight memories of those who occasionally topped the bill there, but there were dozens of other stories. Suffice to say that over the eight years of my theatre apostolate, rarely a week would pass without some worthwhile opportunity to help some struggling, comparatively unknown performer. Indeed, some of the minor supporting acts would appear very regularly. Often they would stay in Sunderland because of the excellent stage digs available there, even when they were working in Newcastle. 'The Tumbling Tomboys', Thelma Seaton and Maureen O'Dell, were both converts to Catholicism when I came across them, and they impressed me hugely by their down-to-earth spirituality. In a very difficult profession, they aimed at daily Mass wherever they were appearing, and managed to make a 'prayer' of their nightly, acrobatic athleticism! Once in Sunderland, they worked on the same bill as Harry Secombe - Harry, in his earlier days, was more comedian than singer. He was one of the most naturally funny and exuberant men it has ever been my privilege to meet in a dressing room. He had a brother who was a vicar, and he had me and some other dressing-room visitors nearly ill with laughter at his stories - then he went on stage and did the same thing for his paying audience.

A FINAL MEMORY - DEIDRE O'CALLAGHAN

Deidre O'Callaghan is a name that has been topping bills in Ireland for close on forty years. In 1958 as a young nineteen-year-old she invaded England, and conquered audiences wherever she appeared. Her classic, dark, Irish beauty, coupled with her expertise on the harp made her a very popular act on the British variety circuit.

In 1958 she came to the Sunderland Empire and, apart from charming the Sunderland folk, absolutely 'bewitched' my priest friends Father Leo and Father Mark. We met again in London the following year when I was visiting Val Doonican and his mother in Lewisham - unfortunately, it was going to take the Pope to get us together again!

Feeling thoroughly ashamed that I had never got over to Ireland to meet the O'Callaghan family, I finally made it for that memorable weekend when John Paul II was to say the biggest Mass (numerically) ever said. Deidre had married famous Olympic athlete Noel Carroll and they now had four children. Noel was the Chief Executive to Dublin City Council and so he was involved in the logistics of the Phoenix Park Mass and the Mansion House reception for the bishops. I had a wonderful few days with the family . . . even managed to squeeze in a game of tennis with Deidre, who had taken up the game seriously after having her four children. I managed to get to Phoenix Park that Sunday and was one of the 1.3 million.

Deidre was still working regularly and starring in cabarets at Dublin's most prestigious hotels. Now she concentrates on being one of Dublin's foremost hostesses. Noel has left the City Council and has become Chief Executive to the Dublin Chamber of Commerce. Last October I had the pleasure of following Peter Ustinov as their weekend guest.

The children of the 1979 Papal visit are now all grown up and Deidre has revelled in the opportunities of changing the harp for the pen. Thomas Moore, the author of *The Last Rose of Summer* and *Believe Me If All Those Endearing Young Charms*, was the inspiration of her MA thesis but she still enjoys her recitals on the harp.

CHAPTER XXII

BISHOP CUNNINGHAM

I have mentioned earlier that my 'first' bishop never actually spoke to me in my first ten years as a priest. My second bishop, Bishop James Cunningham, was quite the opposite! He came to the diocese from Manchester and within eighteen months of his arrival, as Auxiliary Bishop, he seemed to have got to know nearly every priest by name. Suddenly, the bishop was no longer a distant, vague figure who simply wrote letters from the stronghold of Bishop's House in Newcastle, and travelled out to confirmations. Suddenly, he was a man who was everywhere; a man who realized also that the telephone was an invention to be used by bishops as well as by priests. By the time he finally took over the reins of the diocese in 1958, he seemed to have been here for ever, instead of just for eighteen months.

During the time he was Bishop-in-waiting - Co-adjutor, as we call it - an approach was made to me by the Director of the Catholic Missionary Society, Father Ripley, in London, to see whether I would be interested in joining them for a fixed period. This method of recruitment had been customary since Cardinal Heenan had been its first director. Having sounded out a priest, the Society would then ask the diocesan bishop to release him for three to five years. I had replied to Father Ripley that I would be happy to join them if they could arrange it with my bishop. Unfortunately, Bishop Cunningham, who was a canon lawyer by priestly profession, was unhappy with this practice. He told me in no uncertain terms, that *he* would decide who he would send!

One other incident further tested Bishop Cunningham's goodwill towards his Sunderland curate. During my Catholic Stage Guild apostolate in 1954, I had met two unknown performers called Terry O'Neill and Peggy. Terry had married his wife Peggy in the register office, and they had two young, unbaptized children. Travelling around the country for fifty weeks a year had made it very difficult for them either to marry in the church, or persuade a priest on their travels to baptize their children, but during their week at Sunderland Empire, I had a whole seven days to help. I spent many hours with them both, and by means of urgent phone calls and letters, managed to prepare the ground for a convalidation of their marriage. The documentation needed in 1954 had all been carried out, and Bishop McCormack had issued the official dispensation, which arrived on the Saturday morning before Terry and Peggy were due to leave Sunderland. I baptized their two young children on the Saturday afternoon and they renewed their marriage vows in St Mary's after the second-house show on Saturday night. I remember that Terry was struggling with a temperature of 103 degrees at the time!

Convalidations of marriage were still an important part of priestly work in 1954 - possibly, it might have remained just a routine, pastoral statistic, if Terry O'Neill had not become a household name in the north-east of England three or four years later. By 1957-8, Tyne Tees Television were providing the *One O'clock Show* several times a week and it was tremendously popular. This was at a time when daytime television was still almost non-existent. Terry O'Neill, aided by Austin Steele, Jack Haig and others, became the mainstays of this much-loved show.

Quite innocently, Terry had passed on the story to the *TV Times*, the Tyne Tees programme magazine, and it appeared with the heading 'I marry Peggy a second time'. The canon lawyer in Bishop Cunningham was quite affronted by this headline! He was scheduled to come to St Mary's the following Sunday afternoon for confirmation and visitation and he arrived there about thirty-five minutes before the ceremony was due to start. Immediately, he demanded to see the documentation for the O'Neill convalidation. Now, Father Dan's filing system was, at best, somewhat ad hoc, and relied on a dusty alcove off his study. Father Dan knew that the papers had actually been filed after Bishop McCormack's dispensation had been obtained, however, he couldn't find them immediately, and his task was not made any easier by Bishop Cunningham hovering behind him. Moreover, Father Dan was acutely aware that there were seven hundred people in church waiting for a confirmation service! Finally, the confirmation was over and Bishop Cunningham returned to the fray. Eventually, he questioned me, but I assured him that the full procedure for a marriage convalidation had been followed and that a dispensation had been issued by his predecessor several years before. By the time poor Father Dan had eventually found the elusive documents, I knew that my days at St Mary's were numbered!

Within weeks, Bishop Cunningham had telephoned my boss, Father Dan, and told him I must be unhappy in Sunderland, and he proposed transferring me to a priest in Newcastle, who considered that curates were 'expendable commodities'. Indeed, he had already worked his way through a couple of dozen of these commodities and thirsted for more! Father Dan assured Bishop Cunningham that I was actually very happy at St Mary's and he didn't want to lose me . . . so on this occasion, the axe fell on some other unfortunate victim instead. Less than a year later, however, in the next 'Autumn Manoeuvres' - most mass movements of parish priests and curates usually took place at the end of August or beginning of September - Father Dan was informed by telephone that I would be moving in October to St Patrick's, Dipton. On this occasion, Father Dan was quite unable to deflect Bishop Cunningham. I was later to find out that the last curate at Dipton had returned to Ireland suffering from 'nervous exhaustion'. After his recovery, his doctors had suggested to the bishop that he must not return to the same parish! The scene was set for my third placement as a curate.

CHAPTER XXIII

ST PATRICK'S, DIPTON - 15 OCTOBER 1960 TO 16 JULY 1966

If I had found the leaving of my first parish in Darlington traumatic, I found my departure from Sunderland for Dipton even more shattering. And yet, I suppose there was an inevitability about it that somehow soon softened the blow. I had spent nine wonderful years at St Mary's - a long spell for any curate in those days. After the bustle and noise of the busiest street in Sunderland, St Patrick's had a silence that was almost palpable. The parish was situated nearly a thousand feet up in the hills of north-west Durham. It was prone to very frequent hill fog, and in the winter the snow could linger there from November until April or May. There were no hospitals or institutions to look after, but the people were a hardy breed of mining stock, whose strong faith was typical of north-west Durham. I knew that the myriad demands of a downtown city parish like St Mary's would be sadly missing in my new habitat. However, I was sufficiently spiritually focused to realize that this was what God wanted for me at this stage of my priesthood. Somehow, this quickly gave me an indescribable calm that was strengthened by the anticipation of getting to know all the people in and around those hills and valleys.

My new parish priest, Father Cuthbert Duffy, was pleased to welcome me after several months without a curate. He had *something* in common with me: we had both been born in Hartlepool. He had arrived at Dipton after wartime service as an army chaplain, which had taken its toll on him, and had left him highly-strung and introspective. I suspect that he found it very difficult to relate to these 'salt of the earth' miners, their wives and families. He had to rely very much on his curate to act as a liaison, and occasionally, as a buffer between the presbytery and the people.

After the Mass on my first Sunday there, I went to the back of the church and stood on the steps to greet the people as they left. Among the friendly crowd was a smiling, wavy-haired man of about forty who sidled up to me to shake hands and to welcome me. He said, 'I was the outside-left who finally got that goal past you in the one-all draw in the 1949 Universe Cup!' Charlie Errington, it was, and we immediately became friends - a friendship that would only end when I bade farewell to him at his funeral in 1985.

'ROVER' AND THE THOMPSONS

During my last years in Sunderland, I had a collie-retriever called Rover. My mother, who had moved south after my father's death, had kept on my sister Mary's apartment in Mowbray Close, Sunderland. She wanted to have a place in the North-East where she could spend some of her time near me. After her marriage in St Mary's, my sister Mary had moved into my mother's house near Worthing. My new brother-in-law, Jim Kennedy, worked in the City as a shipping broker, and it was just 'commutable'. My other sister, Pauline, had already left the North-East to marry Roy Parker, a Londoner, some years earlier. Rover was a 'family heirloom' originally brought home by Pauline, but then passed on to Mary, and after Mary's departure, left to my mother and myself. Needless to say, as soon as children appeared on the scene, my mother, quite naturally, wanted to spend more time with my sisters in the South, so Rover became my responsibility. During my St Mary's days, with the help of my dear friends, Joan and Les Farquhar, who were just married and living in part of the large Mowbray Close apartment, Rover was never a problem. But when I was transferred to Dipton, I obviously had to transfer Rover with me. I couldn't bring him to the presbytery - Father Duffy and the housekeeper, Hilda, already had a female poodle and spaniel in the house.

So Rover was 'boarded out' in my new parish. After a brief stay with a kindly soul called Winnie Robson next to the presbytery, he later found a permanent lodging with Mary Thompson, a parishioner in Lily Gardens, Dipton. Mary was one of those wonderfully capable women, occasionally to be found in our parishes, who never said no to the priest or the church! She was one of the mainstays in the Catholic Women's League, was the treasurer and buyer for the Annual Garden Fête and Fayre, and a number of other things. She had also organized the cleaning of both church and convent for years. Nothing was ever a trouble to Mary - she was an absolute gem! Mary's daughter, Vera, was frequently delegated to walk Rover after her work if I had not taken him out during the day. Any grumbles from her were met with the reminder from her mother that 'it was the priest's dog after all.' More about Mary and her partner in crime, Kitty Gallagher, later.

I soon achieved a certain celebrity among the forty-plus generation at Dipton as the 'Darlington Priest' who had been responsible for the exit of 'The Pats' - as Dipton, St Patrick's were known - in the 1949-50 Universe Cup. Dipton had never really recovered from that disappointment, so I was under immediate pressure to enter a team for the 1960 competition, which I did. However, we were restricted insofar as the outstanding young players in the parish were already signed for local teams. Indeed, some of them were receiving worthwhile 'expenses' for their Saturday afternoon labours. The players we got together were mainly in the twilight of their careers, or were very young lads with more zest than skill! After a speedy exit from the Cup, it was clear to me that I had to persuade some of the 'stars' of the parish football scene to form a parish team which could compete in a good league. Some of the veterans of the 1949 campaign rallied round and we soon had an enthusiastic committee. Charlie Errington, Mattie Gowland, Pat and Gerard Cunningham and Joe Walker (later to become Durham County Council's Chairman) were very much to the fore, and they helped me to recruit some of the outstanding young players of the area. Our first season in the Durham Central League, a semi-professional league, was a testing time and we rather struggled. However, in our next season, we 'went for broke', and successfully sought admission to the Northern Alliance which was very much a league of ex-professionals and talented youngsters. Teams like Alnwick Town, Amble, Morpeth Town and Bedlington all had excellent grounds and plenty of resources. Needless to say, we could not afford a private coach for our away games. Our transport was usually my blue Ford Escort van, complete with a mattress, plus two or three private cars. Our young players, though sometimes outclassed, gradually matured.

They were playing against teams who 'wanted to play football', and the experience helped develop their own talents. They grew in confidence as the season wore on. Since the number of teams in the League was comparatively small, we were able to enter some of the local cup competitions very successfully. Also we were now able to make our bid to win the Durham County Catholic Cup or the Universe Cup, as it was known. I was well aware that some of my 'stars' like Brian Cunningham, Maxie McAloon, Des Bell, Phil McNulty and Kevin McMahon were all sacrificing lucrative 'expenses' with well-known teams out of loyalty to me! Their lead inspired others like Kevin Cunningham, Joe Lynch, Billy Watkyn, George Cassidy and others, to develop into very sound players.

Even though I had to act as manager, coach, secretary, trainer, cheerleader and, occasionally, player, we had some wonderful times together! At forty I was still fairly fit, thank God. However, on the two occasions when we arrived at Morpeth and Alnwick with only ten men, I could not persuade my goalkeeper, Phil McNulty, to let me take over in goal. Once at Morpeth Town's ground I pleaded with 'Huck' - Phil's nickname to his friends - to let me play goalkeeper and him centre forward. 'Thu's fitter than I am, Father,' coaxed Phil. So I had to get changed and bob around as the solitary man up front. Probably due to the complacency of the Morpeth defence, I was presented with a couple of rather scrambled goals, much against the run of play. In the last ten minutes, as Morpeth felt the game slipping away from them, they lost confidence and I was provided with a 'dream' cross from right-winger, Joe Lynch. I headed the one and only hat-trick of my career! Recently, when I was the guest of Durham County Council Chairman, Joe Walker, at an Aldermans' Day at the Riverside Cricket Ground in Chester-le-Street, Joe was recalling our miracle 5-2 win that day. He still can't believe it and nor, for that matter, can I!

My first visit to Dipton in 1949 was to play in the Universe Cup, and my last official job as manager in 1966 was to lead out the victorious Dipton 'St Pat's' team as winners once again. A huge rivalry had developed from 1962 to 1966 between the diocese's leading teams - Hartlepool St Joseph's, Ushaw Moor St Joseph's, Wingate St Mary's, Birtley St Joseph's and Dipton St Patrick's. We were allowed to play 'guests' as long as they were officially 'signed on' and had played a qualifying league game. My friend, Father John Donnelly, who was involved with the Ushaw Moor St Joseph's team when they lost 2-0 to us in the Cup semi-final, spread the story around among my fellow priests: 'Jack Caden had a big centre-half with a beard playing for "The Pat's" that day.' He did not wish to state categorically that it was Charlie Hurley, but the player was about 6'1½" and also had a Cockney accent!

I realized that when I left Dipton for Sedgefield in July 1966 it would be the end of 'The Pats' football team. Most of the lads, as I have stated, played out of loyalty to me and what I put into the club. When I came to Sedgefield, for some years I enjoyed reading about them as they played for Bishop Auckland or Consett or Annfield Plain and other well-known amateur teams. I still have a very handsome 'four-hundred day' clock on my Sedgefield mantlepiece as a reminder of my happy football days at Dipton – a present from the lads in the team.

Dipton parish was completely different in its demands from St Mary's. Apart from visitation of the homes and attending to a much larger number of housebound, there was a calm, hardly ever experienced in Sunderland. The curate in Dipton parish was expected to take on full responsibility for all the parishioners and for all the sick and housebound, as well as the bulk of the church services. This, however, was no great burden, because there were no other demands to distract one from this routine work – after St Mary's I found it all quite leisurely. Despite the prophecies of some of my priest friends that the 'country' would bore me stiff and the frustration drive me mad, I quickly came to terms with it. Indeed, after a couple of weeks, I was actually enjoying it. For nearly ten years, I had never been able to fit all my day's work into the same day. Here, I could not only complete it, but still have time to 'do my own thing' as well. I was able to join a tennis club, in fact, *two* tennis clubs and was able to take an active part in both the competitive side and the social side of the clubs.

Whenever my mother was 'in residence' in Sunderland, I could pop over and spend a little extra time with her. I had acquired a 1946 Hillman Minx for £80 just before I left Sunderland. With the skilful help of a good car mechanic and dear friend of mine, Eddie McGann, we managed to keep it on the road well past its 'scrapyard date'. I suppose that many priests rely heavily on such 'friendly mechanics' in their parishes. Later on, in my more affluent Sedgefield days, Brian Gill, the husband of my nurse friend, Shirley Allen, would ensure that my 'wheels' were always on the road. Eddie was a great character and with his wife, Mary, and daughter, Elaine, made a second home for me in Pennywell on the outskirts of Sunderland. They tended to spoil me completely, whenever my mother was in the South of England.

I quickly came to realize that Father Duffy was never happier than when he had the house to himself. He was a 'hostage' to claustrophobia and of a nervous disposition. Looking back, I think that one of the reasons why we had a fairly peaceful coexistence was that I recognized and respected this preference. Hilda, the housekeeper, was an excellent cook and she looked after me well. She had a lovely house in Barnard Castle, and would frequently disappear with Father Duffy for the 'inside of a week' to keep it aired. In their absence, Minnie Moffatt, a very pleasant lady from Tantobie, would look after me. In the late afternoon, a wonderful old character called Mary Ellen, from Annfield Plain, would come for a couple of hours, ostensibly to make my tea. Life was indeed pleasant and remained so for a couple of years. Towards the end of that time, Father Duffy began to suffer more and more from his duodenal ulcers. His efforts to counteract the pain by continually drinking pints of milk resulted in less pain but also in increasing his weight! If only Zantac had been invented at that time, it might have changed his life. Finally, he had to undergo major surgery in Shotley Bridge Hospital - surgery which nearly proved fatal. Church services had always been something of an ordeal for him, but after his operation he could not attempt them at all. Consequently, we had a series of supply priests for most of the next two years from Minsteracres Monastery and other sources, while he convalesced. Gradually, I was able to coax him into trying to say a private Mass again and eventually he felt he could face a Sunday congregation once more.

CHAPTER XXIV

FIRE AT ST PATRICK'S

Father Duffy had made a fairly good recovery and went away for a holiday. It was during this holiday that a tragic event was to change the face of St Patrick's Church for ever. The church, like several other churches in the diocese, had originally been made of wood and cast iron. Later, it had been encased in an overcoat of imitation stone to give it a solid, permanent look. A new hall was being added onto our school at the time, and materials and packing cases etc., were stacked very near to the sacristy door of the church.

One morning, at about 2 a.m., I was roused from sleep by a frantic pounding on the front door of the house and the ringing of the bell. I pushed up my window and saw below me a Milk Market lorry driver who was shouting out, 'You're on fire.' Hastily I pulled on my trousers and an anorak, and shot down the stairs. I couldn't see any flames in the house but once I got outside, I saw the church was blazing at *both* ends! I dialled 999, asked for the Fire Brigade and then ran outside to see if I could do anything myself. The duplicate keys to the sacristy and the tabernacle were locked away in Father Duffy's room as he always locked his study and bedroom when he went away. It immediately became obvious to me that the fire was already more or less out of control and I can remember standing helplessly watching the flames leaping along the roof. The separate fires at the sacristy end of the church and at the opposite choir-loft end of the church quickly began to meet in the middle. There was absolutely nothing I could do. The sacristy door was a huge mass of flames and the whole sacristy itself appeared to be already ablaze as I peered through a hole in the burning door. I felt completely isolated and sick with despair as I anxiously scanned the road, watching for the arrival of the Fire Brigade. After what seemed an eternity, they were there and suddenly I was galvanized into action, and answering the questions of the Fire Chief. The dry wood of the original church was blazing uncontrollably within its imitation stone cladding, and despite the heroic efforts of the fire fighters, it was obvious that the flames had too big a hold. The Chief asked me was there anything I needed to rescue from the church. I said I must get to the tabernacle to save 'The Blessed Sacrament'. He gave me a spare fireman's helmet, and we forced our way in through the old boilerhouse door, which was adjacent to the boys' sacristy next to the sanctuary. We then fought our way inside towards the altar itself, while two of his men 'hosed' a jet of water on either side of us! Since we did not have a duplicate key for the tabernacle, he gave me a spare axe, and together we hacked the tabernacle from the burning wood of the altar. With the help of asbestos gloves, we rolled the red-hot tabernacle out of the church by the boiler room door. Since it was red-hot, we had to leave it to cool for half an hour after extra hosing. The tabernacle lock had 'sprung' a little because of the heat, and the Fire Chief had no difficulty in forcing it open for me. The large silver ciborium inside was still intact, with the two hundred consecrated hosts quite recognisable, but stuck together and somewhat charred! I transferred the ciborium to the little convent chapel belonging to our teaching nuns. Since the communion hosts were still recognisable as hosts, but not usable for Holy Communion because they were stuck together by the heat, I had to make several visits to the convent chapel over the next few days. Helped by large quantities of water, I managed to consume the two hundred hosts as reverently as possible, considering the inevitable nausea that would sweep over me after the second or third gulp. It took me five or six visits, but finally the ciborium was empty!

It must have been between 5.30 or 6.00 in the morning when the firemen decided that they could do no more. Much of the roof and the connecting joists of the roof and walls had collapsed. The original wooden frame of the church inside its cement casing had become so dry over the years that it just burnt out like matchwood. Eventually, only the walls remained standing. The smoke billowed out of them as the remains of the original wooden-framed church burned further and further down inside their imitation stone 'overcoat'. Some of the roof joists and their adjoining frames were still intact and kept noisily dripping, evidence of the tremendous efforts of the firemen. The pungent smell of burning was hanging around everywhere and I can remember staring at the stark outline, looking so eerie in the first light of day. I was picturing how different it was from the serene, moonlit, reassuring building that I had seen when I had done my usual check about midnight. Sleep was out of the question and I just watched the fire engines go, feeling numb and dazed! The Fire Chief had warned me that the police and insurance people would soon be here, to say nothing of the press. I made a cup of tea for myself, and sat downstairs in the kitchen waiting for the first intrusion.

Within the hour the police had arrived. They had probably been briefed by the Fire Chief, who had been on the spot early enough to confirm my original observation: that there was a large fire at *both* ends of the church simultaneously right from the discovery of the fire around 2.00 a.m. The police asked me to corroborate this and to assure them that there had been no sign of any fire anywhere at midnight. Clearly they were convinced from the outset that this was arson. The fact that the organ and choir-loft were burnt out even before the firemen had got to work, and that the sacristy at the opposite end of the church was also burnt out at the same stage, pointed to the fact that *two* fires had started at opposite ends of the building some time between midnight and 2.00 a.m. Whoever started the fire had robbed the packing cases near the sacristy door of their straw and packing materials. These had been stacked against the lower part of the sacristy door and set alight; even before the Fire Brigade had arrived I had noticed that the whole bottom half of the sacristy door had burnt through. It was possible to bend down and look straight into the inferno inside. The arsonist had been determined to get the maximum effect as quickly as possible. There was a door leading out of the old boilerhouse to a working sacristy at the side of the sanctuary. This door, unlike the main church door, was not very secure, and I was always aware that it might be forced comparatively easily. This was obviously how the arsonist had got into the church itself. He must have carried an armful of the packing-case straw up to the organ/choir-loft and started a separate fire under the organ itself, which would explain how, immediately after the Milk Marketing driver had aroused me, I could see the fire already blazing at both ends of the building.

During their questioning the police asked me if I knew of anybody who had a grudge against the priest or the Church. I had to say that there could be someone who had a grudge - there would be someone in most parishes - but not the kind of grudge that would incite church arson. I remember well that they asked about one young man by name. The police had stopped him at the nearby crossroads at 1.30 a.m. on the morning of the fire and had questioned him. It just happened that they discovered much later that he had a history of 'church burning' in the area. He was eventually charged with other offences and committed to St Nicholas Psychiatric Hospital in Newcastle for treatment. A year afterwards the Stanley police inspector, who had been on the case, told me that the arsonist admitted several other church fires but refused to admit that he had 'fired' his own church of St Patricks. The inspector said that the coincidence of the crossroads meeting at the time of the blaze, and so near to it, had left them in no doubt about the identity of the arsonist, and the case had been closed. No doubt the fear of reprisals had obviously deterred the culprit from admitting the St Patrick's fire.

Like most churches in our diocese in 1964, we were grossly under-insured. Under later diocesan treasurers this would be rectified, but at that time a total church burn-out would result in a massive debt occasioned by the replacement. The diocese itself took over and lent the money to the church. Between that, and the Restoration Fund efforts, a large, modern, replacement church appeared on the old site. The parishioners responded energetically and generously - most of those early fund-raisers are now resting peacefully in the parish cemetery adjoining the church.

Some, of course, are still alive - I have already told the story of Val Doonican's contribution with his Newcastle City Hall charity concert.

SNOW AND IN PARADISUM

Mention of the parish cemetery reminds me of one of my very first funerals in Dipton. It was the funeral of a dedicated church worker.

Father Duffy asked me to sing a special funeral chant on the way from the church into the cemetery. The chant was a rather plaintive one always sung at Ushaw in our seminary days and was called 'Inparadisum'. The English translation would be something like 'may the angels lead you into paradise etc'. Father Duffy remembered the chant from his Ushaw days so I obliged, thinking it would be a one-off. However, the Dipton folk who heard it that day were rather struck by the poignant sadness of it, and I was constantly asked to sing it at almost every funeral I did for the next five years! If there was the slightest hesitation on my part, I was reminded that I'd done it for so and so's funeral. Sometimes I might be choking with cold, and the snow might be three-foot high at the side of the cemetery path, but I still had to deliver 'just the same'.

Talking of snow, I soon became aware that it was a different world up on Pontop Pyke most winters. My years in downtown Sunderland so close to the sea had shielded me from the reality of winter, but I was soon to find that winters regularly lasted five months or so in Dipton. I was there for a particularly unbelievable one in 1963, when the drifting snow was so sustained and so bad that we were cut off from the surrounding areas for lengthy periods. The main roads into Newcastle, Chester-le-Street and Durham were only just kept open as narrow bus tracks by stints of snow-plough and JCB activity. The result was that for many weeks during that winter there were walls of snow six feet high at either side of the road that went past St Patrick's Church and school. Indeed, the drifting snow was so bad that bus shelters, Ringtons Tea Depot and other landmarks disappeared from view altogether! On the Bosom Bank, winding down to Dipton village itself, people could stand on top of the snow banks and touch the telephone wires and the top of the telegraph pole.

Well into April Diptonians would get unbelieving glances as they ventured into the clean and dry streets of Newcastle still trundling along in their wellies!

My last two years at Dipton were comparatively uneventful ones after the terrible trauma of the church burning. The new school hall was now complete, and we used it for Mass and social events as well as for school use. Father Duffy had recovered well from his surgery and was anxious to promote the Church Restoration Fund. The Catholic

Women's League was very active in fund-raising events, ably led by Mary Bell, Hetty Daly, Mary Wilkinson, Essie Churnside, Kathleen Cunningham, Ella Connelly and others, and, of course, we continued to rely heavily on our annual garden fête and fayre. Mary Thompson and her lieutenant, Kitty Gallagher, were indefatigable workers for the garden fête. Many was the sortie we made together to the wholesalers in Newcastle to satisfy the demands made by the scores of people who had savings clubs for use at garden fête time. It meant a huge amount of bookkeeping and Mary's daughter, Vera, was frequently 'conscripted' to do this side of the work, when she got back after her day's work at Fenwick's Store in Newcastle.

DIPTON YOUTH WORK AND TENNIS

Although I did not have quite the scope for youth work at Dipton, I was nevertheless able to respond to the needs of the young people. We had the football team for the boys and I organized a Catholic Action Training Group for the girls called 'The Grail' with its junior section, 'The Links'. Many a Sunday night we would hire one of Watson's coaches and travel to Horden, Blackhill or Sunderland and other places for Catholic dances organized by their priests. Father Tom Cass of Horden was a pioneer in this field, as was the late Father Paddy Ryan of Blackhill, and Father Tom Burke with his Irish Club in Newcastle. The age grouping of our coach-loads was from 16-25 and the young people loved these outings.

During all my five years at Dipton I have indicated that for the first time in my priesthood I had ample time to 'do my own thing' and I was able to visit Shotley Bridge Tennis Club most Saturdays. There I made many good friends like the local GP, Dr Nayak, himself an excellent tennis player; also Taylor Collinson, the Consett sports outfitter, who was the mainstay of the club. During my Dipton years I was often drafted in for the games of the Dipton Tennis Club. Theirs was a competitive club rather than a social one. For years they ran a team in the Northumberland and Durham First Division - the strongest league in the North-East. An ex-professional footballer, Bob

Vasey, and his wife organized the Club and its teams! Our first pair of Alan Cox and John Herdman nearly always won all their rubbers and gave us a solid start. The final result of the matches would often depend on the fortunes of the third pair. As an occasional part of the third pair, I would struggle to win even one of the six sets we had to play. However, our home courts were made of tarmacadam and were cut out of the side of Pontop Pyke, so the bounce of the ball was high and slow. Some of the top visiting teams would boast county players from the Newcastle area who were accustomed to fast courts. They would often lose their patience on the slow Dipton courts and sometimes throw games away. I was never anything more than a patient, steady player on a tennis court and just occasionally it paid off. I was also introduced to a good tennis club in Newcastle: Vickers Sports Club. I was introduced by Moya Carr, a PE teacher from St Anthony's Grammar School in my Sunderland days. John Archibald and I became regulars as a third pair with Vickers. The standard was not as high as Dipton's, and so we were able to contribute slightly more to the team's success. Here again we were lucky to have a very strong first pair - Little Mac and his partner never dropped a set the whole season. All the excitement would invariably surround John Archibald and myself, and whether we could 'salvage' a couple of sets from the six. Happy days! My partner John eventually became Moya's partner for life, I prepared them for their wedding, and they have been living 'happily ever after' in Rowlands Gill!

SEDGEFIELD - THE BEGINNING

By 1966 I had been eighteen years a curate. The waiting time then to became a parish priest in charge of one's own parish was about twenty years. In 1966 I was to 'lop' a couple of years off the customary twenty years' wait. There was a parish in a place called Sedgefield which was quite unique. During the ten-year period prior to 1966, five different priests had laboured there for varying short periods. The truth was that the parish was no more than a full-time hospitals chaplaincy. As well as a busy District General Hospital, there was a Maternity Hospital, a Geriatric Hostel and a two-thousand bed Psychiatric Hospital. Many priests had served a lengthy hospital apprenticeship during their first twenty years as curates. Understandably, they would have dreams of delegating this responsibility in their turn to their curates, but an appointment to Sedgefield would quickly shatter any such dreams!

The parish itself was a small one - it could bearly afford to support even one priest, let alone two. Most hospitals are situated in towns and cities, and have other churches within a mile or so. Nowadays the 'hospital bleep' can be shared with colleagues, but not then.

In the Sedgefield of 1966 there weren't any hospital bleeps! The nearest town for cover was nearly ten miles away. Psychiatric hospital chaplaincy in 1966 was for most of us a rather daunting prospect. We had received no training whatsoever for hospital chaplaincy, let alone for psychiatric hospital chaplaincy. From 1970 onwards there would be some in-service parish training for deacons and students, but in 1948 there was nothing. Our student days, as I have indicated in an earlier chapter, ended very abruptly at the end of the 'seminary conveyor belt'. The prospect of looking after a 2,000-bed psychiatric hospital was for most priests a very bleak one, hence the steady turnover of Sedgefield parish priests! In mid-1966 it was the turn of the Class of '48 to expect the telephone call that would pre-empt an appointment as parish priest. I had heard on the 'clerical grapevine' that Father Jim Scott of Sedgefield had indicated to Bishop Cunningham during a May visitation that he would appreciate a move away from the heavy demands of the hospitals. The seven priests who were ordained with me on 25 July 1948 were all wondering who might draw the short straw for Sedgefield. The Holy Spirit works in mysterious ways - this is how it was to manifest itself on this occasion!

THE SUNTAN APPOINTMENT

I usually attended a reunion lunch at Ushaw College on the Wednesday of the annual July Grand Week, despite the fact that my own classmates rarely appeared. This time I decided to take my swimming trunks and make use of the excellent swimming baths for a pre-lunch swim. In

July 1966 I drove from Dipton to Ushaw sporting a very healthy suntan. I had taken my mother to Whitburn on the previous Monday and it had been a wonderful, sunny day. Invariably a suntan gives me the healthy look of one whose life expectancy is reasonably assured although sometimes my customary winter pallor would cast doubts on that assumption, and on my fitness and ability to survive real trauma.

As I approached the main steps leading into the college, Bishop Cunningham was engaged in earnest conversation with the Vice-President, Canon Hollis. I mounted-the steps from the other side, trying to avoid any episcopal eye contact – I have never been one to 'chat up' bishops if it could possibly be avoided. His gaze suddenly swivelled in my direction and remained there, so I nodded a passing greeting and continued through the open college door. As I went, I could see his attention was now fixed entirely on me and his animated conversation with the Vice-President was temporarily suspended. I gave a furtive backward look over my shoulder and sure enough, his gaze was still following my passage inside with steady thoughtfulness. As I made for the swimming baths, I suddenly thought to myself, Is he thinking that maybe he has found a solution to the complex Sedgefield appointment question? This fellow, Caden, doesn't look as though he would succumb too readily to the rigorous demands of Sedgefield.

After the lunch, as I drove back to Dipton, I idly wondered whether 'Joss' as we called the bishop, had already got on the phone to Father Scott at Sedgefield and offered him his release. I had guessed correctly, for he had done just that and had phoned Father Scott in mid-afternoon! Needless to say, Jim Scott had immediately accepted his move to Chester-le-Street . . . Joss, however, had insisted that he would ring him back in twenty- four hours. The following day at lunchtime, Joss telephoned me, beginning the conversation with 'Father Scott is moving to Chester-le-Street and I am appointing you as parish priest in Sedgefield.' I was temporarily speechless because as soon as he said 'Father Scott' I could have finished the sentence for him. He then said to me, 'You're not saying much, John . . . it is not the kind of place you will be left for the rest of your life . . . but I am hoping you will stay there for five years.' I just didn't have the heart or the nerve to tell him there was something very much déjà vu about all this!

Father Duffy told me straightaway that he would have been horrified to get such an appointment - something of course I knew already. He was intrigued to know who was coming in my place. Despite the fact that I told him the bishop had not informed me, he was still inclined to think I knew. At lunch the next day when the telephone rang again and the bishop informed him that Father Leo Coughlin was coming, he was not at all happy. Leo and Father D had met only once, and their meeting had certainly been less than cordial.

I found it difficult to convince Father Duffy that I had nothing to do with it. Sadly, 'consultation' should have taken place about the type of person my successor should be. However, typical of the church of the 1960s it never happened. My friend Leo was just as volatile as Father Duffy was, and Leo lasted just three weeks! He was then moved on to Amble, and the 'official' story was that his Dipton move was only temporary.

He was replaced by Father John Brady who had a similar temperament to my own, and was perfect for the job. If only the bishop had consulted me at the time, I would have immediately suggested Father John Brady, but 'consultation' even with a small 'c' was quite unknown at the time. Now, in the 1990s, with Bishop Ambrose it happens all the time.

CHAPTER XXV

SEDGEFIELD - THE EARLY YEARS

I travelled to Sedgefield on 16 July 1966, but I paid an earlier visit to have a formal interview, with Dr Duggan-Keen. Dr Duggan-Keen was the Chief Psychiatrist and Medical Superintendent of Winterton Hospital. 'DK', as he was called, was an eminent psychiatrist and I was immediately impressed by his charm and obvious efficiency. This efficiency was to manifest itself on countless occasions during the next decade when I worked with him or had the opportunity to watch him at work. He had an excellent team of psychiatrists in people like Drs Jack Hawkings, Eric Sutherland, Dr Pilizcek, a Polish expert on the North-East and others. The large phalanx of psychiatrists were helped enormously in those days by their psychiatric social workers. These did most of the background research into the problems of patients, research which often enabled psychiatrists to make very sound diagnoses at a much earlier stage. Later on, psychiatric social workers were compelled to become 'generic' social workers - in my opinion a mistake. In the course of the next ten years the generic social worker had in turn to be redirected to become a 'specialist' social worker.

Gerald Duggan-Keen was soon aware that my district general hospital chaplaincy qualifications were good, but my actual experience of psychiatric chaplaincy was minimal. He assured me that I would be sent on valuable courses in my first year at Winterton and was as good as his word! One of the problems, however, was that I was soon to learn that my other chaplaincy at Sedgefield General Hospital was to be so demanding that I would be compelled to get a resident, 'locum' or 'supply priest' into my house if I were to be absent even for a few days; but more about the demands of the hospitals later.

I have stated already that most priests would have regarded an appointment to Sedgefield - even two years earlier than usual - as drawing the short straw. Strangely I never felt like this at any time during my earlier or later years in Sedgefield. Indeed, I actually felt the opposite. Despite what appeared to be the rather haphazard manner of my 'suntan appointment', I always felt that maybe Bishop Cunningham did actually get it right. From my first weekend there, I was utterly happy in my work. I found the challenge and demands of what was possibly the largest hospital chaplaincy in the country, a recipe for contentment, both spiritual and temporal. I was quite happy again that this was what the Good Lord wanted me to do at that time. The more demands it made on me, then the happier I was!

My mother, who spent a few months of every year in our apartment in Sunderland, agreed to come with me and look after me. At the time she was seventyish, quite fit and an excellent cook. I was well aware that she was very proud of my priesthood, as indeed were many mothers of her generation with regard to their priest sons. The first few weeks went by busily but smoothly. It was essential to have someone manning the telephone twenty-four hours a day. Between the forty wards of Winterton Hospital, and the sixteen-plus busy coronary care unit, of Sedgefield General Hospital, I would spend many hours in the hospitals every day. In 1966 there were no hospital bleeps. Frequently, emergency calls would come from the District General Hospital while I was working somewhere in Winterton.

'Gert' as I used to call my mother, got a new lease of life. She had a very clear insight even then into the Church and its mission. Furthermore, her own experience of having a Protestant Orangeman for a father, and a saintly Irish Catholic for a mother, made her only too well aware of the problems that could arise in any 'mixed marriage'. She loved religious discussions, and I always felt that she had an unerring insight into the workings of the non-Catholic mind. Although very staunch in her Catholic Faith, she nevertheless was an ecumenist long before her time. I can still see her now . . . gently holding the arm of someone she was engaging in discussion, while she continued to round off her argument!

However, after about three months of busy contentment she suddenly became very ill. We had not had time to sign on with a new doctor, so I sought out a Doctor Patrick Skeehan from Kelloe, a well respected Catholic doctor in the area, to come and see her. Dr Skeehan called in one of my consultant physician colleagues from Sedgefield General Hospital, Dr Kenneth Chalmers.

Although I feared the worst, Dr Chalmers was able to treat her successfully for a rare condition called 'temporal arteritis'. It was in the early days of steroids, and these undoubtedly saved her life and her sight. During the weeks that she was ill, it was imperative that I get someone into the house, partly to keep an eye on my mother, and partly to answer the phone for hospital emergencies. My old friend and support in Dipton, Mary Thompson, had sadly died on 1 July, three weeks before I came to Sedgefield. Mary had been greatly interested in what would be my first place as a parish priest, but was not there to see me go to it; or indeed for that matter even to know where it was.

Her daughter Vera had nursed her through her long illness and I heard that Vera was on extended sick leave at home after the death of her mother. Vera's father, Ted, a very active, retired miner, spent most of the day out of the house after his wife's death. I thought it might help Vera psychologically if she got a change of scenery from Lily Gardens, Dipton, so with the full encouragement of her father she agreed to spend three days during the week here, and the remaining four with her father. She settled in very quickly and struck up a very happy relationship with my mother, who was now gradually recovering. Vera was her mother's daughter when it came to church work, and soon became an integral part of the presbytery scene in Sedgefield. Very quickly the three days stretched into most of the week since there was always more than enough work. By the time my mother was back in circulation, she had already come to rely on Vera a great deal. Vera had taken the place of my sisters, who were both bringing up their own families in the South of England, and my mother was anxious that she should stay on.

As I write these lines, that brief 'helping out' period of 1966-7 has stretched to thirty-one years! My old dog, Rover, who had been boarded out with the Thompsons during my Dipton years, made up the third part of the Sedgefield ménage. Gert, as I called my mother, who had quickly adopted Vera, made it clear to me that she didn't want to sit in the dining room ringing bells for attention; so it was agreed that we would eat and relax together as a family. Undoubtedly, this was an unusual arrangement at that time, but even by 1966 very few priests *had* resident housekeepers. Clearly my presbytery was going to be a home rather than a tied cottage where the priest just lived and worked.

MY ATTITUDE TO MY MINISTRY

I have hinted earlier that priesthood after the Vatican Council was, potentially, to be a totally different entity from priesthood before Vatican II. For those who worked as priests for fifteen years prior to that Council, 'ecumenism' had suddenly become one of the 'in' words in ministry. In 1966 I was working a parish with a hundred or so Catholics in a village of a thousand people where hospitals were the main industry. Since I was in and out of Sedgefield General Hospital an average of twenty times every week, and at the same time was trying to make some 'impact' on the 2,000-bed Winterton Psychiatric Hospital, I became one of the most visible people in the community. I was vividly aware that, with such a high profile, most local people would have their idea of Catholicism coloured by the way they saw the Catholic priest interacting in their own community, whether at hospital or village level. And so in my hospital work, for example, I deliberately set out to talk to everybody. Christ's empathy for the sick and the troubled was universal, and not just for the chosen few. Such empathy was fairly straightforward and easily achievable in the old Florence Nightingale-type of twenty-bed ward in Sedgefield General. On my rounds I would go round every bed, and while doing so would make arrangements to minister to those labelled RC at the same time. The cynic might dismiss this as pandering to a personality cult, but that was far from the mark. The truth was that I realized that the better I personally was accepted, then the better what I stood for would be accepted. This was simply an extra dimension of the Church's mission post-Vatican II, but it was also something that I myself had consciously aimed for ever since my 1948 ordination. This had been especially true in regard to youth work and convert instruction work.

As I became better and better known, I saw it as my duty to work to build up the *whole community* in Sedgefield. I joined a group in the village who were anxious to create more amenities for the increasing population. This soon became the Sedgefield Community Association and very successful indeed it was. Two of my parishioners, sisters Margaret Bell and Monica Cunningham, offered themselves successfully for work on the expanding town council; afterwards I was asked to join them also as an independent in 1970. One of the local GPs, Dr Elizabeth Sutherland, joined the town council too about that time. Between us, as a group of newcomers, I think we gave the new town council a new sense of direction which it had possibly rather lacked up to that time. Other new members like Derek Lofthouse and Keith Wells also made valuable contributions, while existing members like Raymond Iceton and the late George Roper were encouraged to play a more dynamic part in the affairs of the council. During those early years of the 1970s the town council was genuinely not political, albeit there were a couple of members who stood under official political colours; but the common good of Sedgefield was very much the important yardstick in debate. The danger can be that when the bottom layer of government becomes a political layer, then it often feels constrained to pay lip service to the top layer - Parliament itself. Really important local issues can then sometimes become clouded, or at worst become mere pawns in a political chess game.

In due course, my early experience of local government at town council level was to result in my election as the County Councillor for Sedgefield Constituency of Durham County Council. In 1973 there was a reorganization of local government. Because of the rapid growth in population in Sedgefield from 1,000 to 5,500, Sedgefield was, for the first time, to have the opportunity to elect its own county councillor. Two senior leaders of the community, Arthur Kell (a former member of the Labour Party and an Independent Methodist Minister) and George Pearson (a former member of the Sedgefield Rural District Council) formally approached me to stand as an Independent Candidate in the 1973 new County Council Elections. They were confident that my position as a community leader in Sedgefield, and my hospital connections, were sufficiently strong to warrant success. I declined, saying I thought my bishop would not approve of it. I did promise them, however, that I would consult him, but I have to confess that I failed to pursue it further. At the eleventh hour, Arthur and George sought me out and asked what the bishop had decided. I can still see the six-foot-two figure of Arthur Kell gently chiding me and suggesting that I should telephone the bishop even at that late stage. Surprisingly, once Bishop Cunningham had been assured that I was not a member of a political party and that there *had* been a precedent in the North-East, both in Middlesbrough and Hartlepool years before, he gave his blessing!

I never realized of course at the time what a quantum leap was involved in the transition from town council to county council. I was quite inexperienced in the political field, but I soon discovered that the world of politics was very much alive at county council level, even though there were at the time two or three Independents on the council. Mainly due to the fact that half the population knew me from my daily work in the hospitals and the community, and because a very supportive group of mostly non-Catholic friends helped organize a campaign for me, I managed to be elected! In retrospect, it was quite unique, and could only have happened in Sedgefield. The years that followed gave me a good insight into the real world of Education, Social Services, and eventually, of Health. Such insight helped me both as a priest and as a community leader.

Naturally, it demanded a huge amount of extra work on my part. However, during my my first four years as a county councillor I was able to help scores of people who needed advice or guidance or both. After gaining their confidence, they would be quick to recommend me to their friends and families. Consequently, when I had to stand for re-election in 1977, I gained a landslide victory which was to be repeated as long as I was still on the scene. I was sufficient of a realist to know that, uniquely, I had created a 'personal vote' that transcended party allegiances, and this vote was largely based on trust!

SEDGEFIELD GENERAL

Meanwhile, my work in the parish and in the hospitals went on as usual. I have implied already that my work in the General Hospital was quite endless in those early years. In the Roman Catholic Diocese of Hexham and Newcastle remuneration from hospital chaplaincy was never personal. The Department of Health contract might be with the individual chaplain, but the salary went to the diocese through the Church. In those days the assessment of salary was often the result of an ad hoc numbers game involving the hospital secretariat. Daily returns from individual wards regarding religious denomination were not always accurate. Often, they could be based on a 'perceived' *average* rather than on reality. If the average number of Catholics in the population was about 10 per cent then often that 10 per cent was equally divided between RCs and Free Church denominations in the final tally that reached the Hospital Secretary. I discovered that the RC remuneration on average at Sedgefield General Hospital was based on half a session - a session at that time was notionally about 3½ hours work. Since the money was not personal to me, I challenged the system. In 1966 a Catholic hospital chaplain was expected to visit any RC who was in any danger at all as frequently as either the hospital authorities or the relatives demanded it. I was still actively fostering this philosophy by regularly lecturing in the nurse training schools. The Department of Health and Whitley Council decided that I should 'log' all calls made outside my sessional two hours per week, and travel expenses should be paid for each additional visit. In this way, every call I made to Sedgefield General Hospital in those years prior to its transfer to North Tees, Stockton, was accurately logged. Hospital Secretary, Ron Owens, was a great help in all this. Suddenly my parishioners were no longer subsidizing their parish priest in his two dozen absences from his church work every week.

Sedgefield General Hospital was a converted wartime hospital. It had only about 300 beds, but these beds were rarely empty. Matron Carr was typical of many hospital matrons of that era, though discipline was not as strict as in my first hospital chaplaincy at the Royal Infirmary, Sunderland. Sedgefield was a Teaching Hospital, and Sister-Tutor, Evelyn Campbell, was a very likeable and popular tutor. We continued our friendship well after her retirement until her untimely death in 1995. Indeed, for many years, 'Ev', as she was known, would insist on my being her 'first foot' on New Year's Eve, despite the fact that by no stretch of the imagination could I have been described as 'dark', one of the usual requirements. Many of her student nurses have remained friends of mine throughout my thirty-one years in

Sedgefield: Rita Grieves, our Sedgefield 'Practice' nurse, Rita Taylor, currently Mayor of Sedgefield, 'Nev' and Sheila Marshall, and 'Crosshills Hotelier' Anne Carr - all have supported me with their friendship.

Another lovely memory: Sedgefield General Hospital staff nurse, Miriam Lonsdale, 'one of Ev's Protégées' - I married her in 1968 to a young Canadian lieutenant, John Boileau. After thirty years of friendship John and Miriam would invite me to be their guest at Canadian High Commission Headquarters in London - by this time the young lieutenant would have risen to the dizzy heights of Colonel and Miltary Adviser!

I have scores of wonderful stories from both my Sedgefield General chaplaincy, and also from my Winterton chaplaincy. Here are one or two from the General:

In the 1970s we priests were trying to bury the old idea of the last rites. After the Vatican Council I always stressed to nurses and others, that the 'Anointing of the Sick', was to help the patient get better rather than to help the patient into eternity! I tried to emphasize this idea in all my lectures in the Nurses' Training School. One evening a young staff nurse friend of mine, Ann Green, was having a very hectic time on her medical ward. All the side wards were full of seriously ill people - they actually even had an overflow onto the main ward. Ann dutifully phoned me and told me there was a Catholic patient very ill indeed in the side ward so within five minutes I was in the foyer of the ward. Ann was halfway down the ward struggling with a drip for some poorly patient. She spotted me and frantically pointed me to the right-hand No. 2 side ward, being too busy to come down the ward to me. I immediately went into the side ward and, crouching over the sick man in the bed, said, 'I'm Father Caden, the Catholic Priest. I've come to give you a special blessing to help you to get better.'

The man was very ill but quite conscious, and I thought he looked at me rather quizzically. I just thought that maybe he hadn't talked to a priest for some time and I proceeded to give him the usual Blessing with the Holy Oil, specially set aside in our religion for the Blessing of the Sick. I asked him to say the Our Father with me and he joined in it fairly audibly. At that moment one of the doctors came in to check his chart, so I vacated the side ward with a friendly wave. As I came out into the foyer, I almost collided with Staff Nurse Ann who blurted out to me, 'Sorry, Father, I pointed you to the wrong side ward . . . that's Mr Alexander, he is not a Catholic! It's Mr Harrison who is the Catholic; he is in the other side ward.' So I duly went into the other side ward and gave the Blessing of the Sick to Mr Harrison as well. Happily, they both got better, and in due course went home in time for Christmas!

Several months later I was at one of the checkouts in Stockton ASDA with my mother and a trolley full of shopping. My mother said to me, 'John, there's a man at that far checkout and he is waving to us.' I looked at him, but although the face was familiar I did not recognize him. At first I thought he must have been waving to someone behind me, but no, he was still waving excitedly at me. As I came away from my checkout he rushed over to me, shook hands and said, 'It's great to see you again Father Caden, I'm Mr Alexander. Sedgefield General Hospital? You gave me that blessing. My wife knows now that if I ever have to go back, she has to telephone for you to give me that blessing again!'

The other story concerns me as a patient! One morning I had gone in to the Coronary Care Unit on Ward One to take Holy Communion to one of the three patients there. I gave the man Holy Communion and was about to leave the ward, when I experienced some sharp, sudden chest pain. Sister Esther Hume, the no-nonsense sister-in-charge, noticed my deathly pallor and my grimaces of pain. She steered me into her office, sat me down and saw that I was sweating profusely, so she gave me a drink of water to revive me. I told her I would be alright and that I was driving over to Sunderland with some second-hand clothes for the Little Sisters of the Poor. She informed me that I would 'not be b— well driving anywhere', and that I must stay there in her office until she sent up the corridor to bring down Dr Chalmers from Ward Six to have a look at me! Within twenty minutes I was occupying the fourth Coronary Care Unit bed . . . all wired up and monitored like the patient I had just visited half an hour before! Once I was settled in, they gave me some medication. The pain disappeared and I felt rather drowsy. Within about half an hour Dr

Chalmers arrived at the ward with two of his trainee doctors or 'housemen' as we called them - in this case two lady doctors. After saying to me: 'Do you feel a little better, Father?' he smiled; waving imperiously at me in the bed, he continued, 'Ladies, this is a classical case of a slight coronary episode.' His supplementary diagnoses were lost on me, because I must have drifted off with the effects of the Valium. I was a patient then in my own hospital for about five days. Sister Hume always kept would-be visitors at bay, but when she was off duty I would be exhausted by the time we got to about 4.00 p.m. I learned later that my coronary was probably marginal. The SGOTs *did* indicate a coronary episode, but only a slight one; which was exactly what my friend Dr Chalmers had said when addressing his students!

I was only forty-seven at the time, and psychologically felt that my whole world had suddenly collapsed. Later, I was helped enormously by the positive assurance of my physician friend, 'You must be confident, Father . . . you will not be an invalid, and you will be playing tennis again within a few months, but always remember, you must only try to play at eighty per cent of your previous output. Once you feel tired, stop! Don't let your competitive spirit push you any further.' It was the soundest advice I ever got from a doctor. Furthermore, the rough treatment I received from my friend, Sister Esther, possibly saved my life.

WINTERTON

Winterton Hospital, like most psychiatric hospitals, provided scores of stories, some predictable, others tragic, others quite unique. As I write this after thirty-one years working at the 'coalface' as it were, in Winterton Psychiatric Hospital, I cannot speak too highly about the high standards of care in what was for a couple of decades the largest psychiatric hospital in Europe. Hundreds of patients in my early years of work there had virtually been abandoned by their families, so serious had been the stigma of mental illness in the first half of this century. It was the nursing staff and the ancillary staff who so often took the place of those families and became 'family' to so many of the patients.

Inevitably, most of the older ones became 'institutionalized', even the most intelligent of them. Some patients who were there in the 1950s and 1960s should never have been in a psychiatric hospital. The philosophy of successive governments 'to get them back into the community' was understandable, and perhaps sometimes quite laudable. However, by the time 'Care in the Community' became a reality in the last fifteen years, there was never going to be sufficient funding in the NHS to achieve it properly. Mental illness had always been the Cinderella of the Health Service, and funding to achieve universal care in the community was never sufficient.

To the knowledgeable in psychiatry, it was never going to be a cheaper option than continuing to run the existing psychiatric hospitals. Sadly, some politicians thought that this could *still* be achieved, even with the dwindling funding percentages of NHS Psychiatry. They were sometimes proved to be tragically wrong, especially when some of the newer chief executives were people more conversant with the ethic of the business world than with the tragedy of mental illness. Once the timescale of Care in the Community became strongly governed by the ideology of politicians, then tragic mistakes were simply bound to happen. During the last ten years it took these tragedies to *slow up* the headlong impetus already achieved in the earlier years. It might not be too cynical to suggest that the possible eventual effect at the ballot box was often the reason for slowing down the process to an acceptable level!

But enough of my musing on the efficacy of Care in the Community. One of my earlier memories of Winterton was somewhat tragic in its denouement. Within a year of my arrival as Chaplain I came across a lady who had been one of my youth club girls in my first Darlington parish in 1950. She had married in the 1950s, had shown symptoms of schizophrenia and had been admitted to Winterton in due course. Teresa, I will call her, had achieved some fame in the hospital by the time I had got to know my way around the forty wards in 1967 and had renewed my acquaintance with her. Because she had known me as a sixteen-year-old, once she had run me to earth, she made it clear to all and sundry that she had some kind of 'proprietary rights'. The new chaplain was 'her priest'! When I went in for my weekly confessional sessions every Saturday morning, Teresa would be directing traffic, and would insist that I spend the last quarter of an hour with her. She was a blithe spirit, and quite uninhibited. Her psychiatrist at the time kept her on the opposite side of any fluctuating depression with antidepressants. 'Ebullient' was the description that readily comes to mind to describe her more frequent mood swings. Teresa was usually a fairly happy person, and she must have impressed her psychiatrist and the medical board. In due course they arranged for her to try out a job in Yorkshire, in a police hostel at some police headquarters. From my own knowledge of Teresa it was not the most inspired piece of community care philosophy, even for twenty-five years ago. Within a few days it proved to be a complete disaster! About five days after her arrival at the police headquarters, Teresa had run away and hitch-hiked back to Sedgefield. At about 8 p.m. she duly arrived, pounding on my door, looking wild and disturbed. She swept straight into my study demanding a cigarette and a cup of tea. It took me about half an hour to calm her down. She then asked me if I would take her back to the ward. I telephoned the ward, which was a separate, villa-type ward, and told them I would be delivering her back shortly. My mother, in her prudence, insisted that Vera should go up to the hospital with us in the car. On the way up to the hospital Teresa was fairly calm, and I thought she would be quietly readmitted by the Duty Doctor. I took her into the ward which by this time had only the two night nurses who had come on duty at about 8.30 p.m. They told me to leave her with them since the Doctor was expected.

What transpired afterwards I only learnt the next day. Apparently the Duty Doctor was seriously delayed. Teresa began to get restless and had some altercation with one of the night nurses. Now I should have told you that even as a 16-year-old schoolgirl, Teresa was an unusually powerful girl and as a 38-year-old woman she was no less powerful! Following the altercation, Teresa had grabbed the poor night nurse and pinned her to the floor. In the ensuing struggle she dragged her by the hair around the large ward-dormitory. She then overpowered the other nurse who tried to intervene. For another quarter of an hour there was absolute chaos and panic before the helpless nurses and the terrified patients were rescued by the arrival of the male Duty Doctor. He immediately telephoned the Night Superintendent to summon aid, and Teresa was taken off to the female ward which housed the padded cells at that time.

Few people under fifty today would ever have seen a padded cell - they actually disappeared over twenty-five years ago. It was simply a small, secure room which was upholstered from floor to ceiling. The occupant, clothed in a simple garment, was quite unable to do any damage to him/herself or anyone else. The patient was monitored continually and fed at the normal times. Thank God, that a quarter of a century later, with more sophisticated drugs available, these padded cells have disappeared altogether. On this occasion, Teresa spent a few days there and her medication was carefully monitored; quite obviously she had not taken any medication while at the police headquarters! A week later she appeared all smiles at my Saturday morning confession venue. She said, 'I believe I said some terrible things about you to the nurses when I was in the "pads".' Teresa had been letting rip with her fantasies! 'I'm sorry, Father,' she continued, 'I don't believe I said some of the things they say I did, but I want us to be friends again . . .' After that episode, Teresa must have had a change of psychiatrist - who believed in keeping her potential mania so controlled that she became more and more depressed and introverted. She disappeared from Winterton in one of the Community Care manoeuvres and I have lost contact with her.

I will shortly tell another story of Winterton which is a much happier one - indeed it is so memorable, it deserves to have a chapter all to itself: the story of Ernie. However, there were scores of other memories - Patsy, who used to swallow safety pins and loved to come down to my house most Saturday mornings to have a cup of tea with 'Gert' and Vera. As indeed did Margaret - she had emptied a pan of boiling stew over her bullying husband and had been sent to Broadmoor. Later she had been transferred to Winterton to be nearer her relatives. Margaret was a charming lady who probably was so provoked thirty years before that she had been driven to the extreme. In my book, she was never mentally ill in the accepted sense of the term. Needless to say, in 1966 there were scores of patients who were victims and casualties of the First World War - men who had 'broken under the strain of the Somme' or who had suffered from gas warfare. There were one or two ladies who had only been 'guilty' of having a baby outside of wedlock . . . and had then been obstracized by their families. They had subsequently languished in a psychiatric hospital for the next thirty to forty years and had become completely institutionalized. Indeed, these and many other examples make the case for Care in the Community both for mental illness and mental abnormality a top priority. I remember Health Minister Enoch Powell nearly forty years ago floating the concept without any great success. Successive health ministers tried and failed in their turn. Eventually, it all happened too late and often with too little money to achieve it. But we all know that it had to happen. Let's learn the lessons and build on them for the future.

ERNIE

In 1966 I inherited Ernie Broadley as a church organist at St John Fisher. Ernie was a convert to Catholicism prior to my arrival and was a brilliant musician. He had, I understand, shown signs of schizophrenia in the 1930s, lived in Darlington and was a LRAM and teacher of music. However, his small income failed completely to take care of his wife and four children, and he was too proud of his profession to accept the dole - the income support of the 1930s. He also became obsessive about religion and tried to convert to Catholicism with secret visits to St Augustine's in Darlington. In the midst of his struggle to find God and to cope with his failure to support his family, Ernie was committed to Winterton Hospital in 1933. Thirty years later he told me that he stopped his wife coming to see him - he thought in his paranoia at the time that she was merely posturing. The result was that he completely lost contact with his wife and his children for many years.

When I arrived in Sedgefield in 1966 Ernie was already church organist at St John Fisher and the church had become his life. He would make ten visits a week here, and would not only provide music on every occasion, but would delight in providing a reading as well. The curtain that had been drawn over his domestic life was offset by his almost obsessive involvement with the Church. By 1970 when I had helped to set up a Community Association in Sedgefield, Ernie would come down to the village to take part in the Drama Society, the Chess Club, the History Society and any other groups that took his fancy. He would also make frequent visits to my house to take in programmes like *Mastermind* and the occasional opera or symphony on television. About the year 1973 George Atkinson, a visionary chief nursing officer at Winterton, approached me about him. George said, 'The psychiatrists think that Broadley should go into a hostel in Darlington. He certainly could qualify, since he has not been on any medication for several years. But I think it would be a serious mistake. The hospital has become his home. He leads a much fuller life than most people living in Sedgefield. So long as he has Winterton as a base, he can enjoy a quality of life outside the hospital that is unique. What do you think, Father?' I assured him that, as Chaplain, I would give him complete support. Ernie stayed and enjoyed another twenty years in his adopted home. Admittedly, he had to some extent become institutionalized, but this was the right decision for Ernie. In due course I arranged with a caring charge nurse, Ken Saiger, that we would provide a small coloured TV for Ernie to use in his private room. By that time hospital numbers had been reduced to about 1,200 patients and a huge modernization programme was in place on the two-square-mile site. Ernie revelled in all the more highbrow TV programmes which sadly he usually had to miss on the ward TV.

I have stated that Ernie was a musician, indeed one of the most brilliant musicians I have ever met. If I hummed a tune for him, even though he had never even heard it previously, within a couple of minutes he could be embellishing it like the maestro he was.

Occasionally, in those days, I was in demand to sing at charity concerts connected with the community or the Church. To me Ernie was a godsend. My bass/baritone demanded the use of keys that often were not available in commercial sheet music. Ernie could provide a sweeping accompaniment without any sheet music at all. Anything from 'The Gendarmes Duet' to 'There's a Hole in the Bucket, Dear Liza' came easily to him. I never had to worry about sheet music. The former piece I sometimes did with Arthur Kell, who was my instigator onto the County Council, remember; the latter piece I did with Lynn Clayton, who after thrilling local audiences here in Sedgefield with her acting, went on to achieve national fame as a professional actress! When Lynn and I meet up in London where she lives, we love to reminisce about Ernie, and about his outings with the Sedgefield Players who have been wonderfully led by Walter Howell for twenty-five years. We laugh about the night that Ernie musically encouraged Lynn to portray such annoyance with my 'Henry' that her 'Liza' almost swept me completely off the small stage!

Just one other story about Ernie - although there are scores of them. One night I was engaged as a free cabaret by some of the Middlesbrough churches who were launching a Planned Giving Campaign. It was to be held at the then very posh Marton Country Club. I was to provide the cabaret for the 'oldies' together with the 'commercial' to launch the campaign. This was to be followed by the main event for the younger people - a dance with music provided by the excellent resident orchestra. I did some popular ballads like 'If I could Help Somebody', 'Old Man River' and several others. Ernie was dressed to suit the occasion - dicky bow and all! The applause had barely died away when the orchestra was ready to start up. Ernie loved to dance and at seventy-three was as nimble as anyone half his age. As I sat watching him sip a lager and lime, I could see his feet were tapping the floor very meaningfully. I asked him whether he would like a dance or two before we set off back for the hospital. He nodded vigorously but I could see that most people were in their parties! I realized Ernie would not have the confidence to go up to strangers and ask for a dance so I quietly slipped over to a nearby table where three ladies were sitting, apparently without partners. I noticed that they had been there for the cabaret so I told them my pianist loved dancing, but he had no partner and was shy to ask anyone. I wondered whether they would oblige, and they assured me that they would be delighted to do so! I pointed them out to Ernie and suggested to him that the small, dark one was about his size. As the orchestra opened up Ernie was away like a whippet, but to my surprise, he ignored my advice. Instead he chose the biggest lady of the three, who was a rather well-endowed blonde. Ernie was a small, dapper man and she must have been at least three inches taller in her stilettos. Nevertheless, he set about his steps like a thoughtful Fred Astaire and clearly enjoyed every second of the dance. As

Caricature - Ernie dancing with 'Dolly Parton'

he returned to our table I just had time to whisper to him, 'Now give them all a dance, Ernie', when I was accosted by some old friends from my Middlesbrough student days. The orchestra was striking up the chords of the next dance when Ernie darted off again before any other people had reached the floor. Ignoring my advice, he made a beeline once again for the 'Dolly Parton' of the nearby table trio. Each time I was distracted with old friends from my Middlesbrough days, Ernie never missed the opportunity to slip onto the floor. I had promised Ken Saiger that I would have him back to the ward by midnight. After two or three unsuccessful attempts to lure him from the dance floor, I was eventually speeding back to Winterton with my musical Cinderella. I saw him safely back to his ward at about ten past midnight where the night nurse had some hot milk ready for him before he retired. During the next few days Ernie told me several times how much he had enjoyed the whole night.

Ernie died on 27 June 1991, two days before his ninetieth birthday. I never knew any man who had such a zest for life! I worked out that in his thirty-five years association with St John Fisher Church, he must have made twenty-thousand journeys from the hospital to the church. He had a wonderful relationship with God, which often left me as a priest struggling with the world and its distractions, sometimes rather envious of his rock-like faith. He was ill only a few days before dying after surgery in Bishop Auckland General Hospital. At the time I was on holiday in Benidorm with my sister Mary and brother-in-law Jim. Vera telephoned me to say that Ernie was dying. Thomsons would only fly me back if it was a case of life and death of a *relative*.

A friendly Thomsons' rep suggested to me eventually that if *I* had to fly back for 'medical treatment', then they would accept that reason. Now I had just pulled a hamstring while playing tennis with Padre Jordi, the local curate and a doctor friend of his. Our doctor friend duly obliged me with the necessary medical certificate. Ernie had become 'family' to me, and I simply *had* to be there to lead my parishioners in celebrating the life of this most remarkable man. We gave him a wonderful 'send-off' in St John Fisher. Three of his four children who had been reunited with him during the previous twenty years were all there to take an active part in his funeral service. His granddaughter Stella did the reading at the Requiem Mass. Len, Ernie's eldest son, who had taken on the role of father to his younger brothers way back in 1937 when Ernie had entered Winterton, got the family together for the occasion. Eric, Ernie's son in Canada, was unable to get over, but subsequently came to see his father's burial place and headstone. Ernie bequeathed a small legacy to his beloved St John Fisher Church - I thought that the most fitting memorial to him would be a new organ, so I put his legacy towards a new electric organ which now bears a plaque. The inscription on the plaque reads: 'To the memory of Ernest Broadley LRAM, St John Fisher Organist from 1960 to 1991'.

THE COUNTY COUNCIL

My busy life as a parish priest, hospitals chaplain and now county councillor and town councillor went on with never enough hours in the day. I have stated earlier that my political experience was nil but even though I was elected as an Independent, and was not a member of any political party, I was mixing, often three days a week, at County Hall, with seventy-two people who were mostly really professional politicians. From the beginning I made a rule for myself that in any debate on Education or Social Services - my committees - I would always be consciously objective. I never thought of myself on a Socialist-dominated County Council as one of the opposition.

In 1973 there was a group of six Liberals elected who were mainly young politicians with 'busy day jobs'. They regarded themselves very much as the official opposition since there were only two Conservatives elected on the council. The old North-East Labour Party of the 1950s and 1960s had occasionally clouded their record by alleged abuses of power. The new Labour Group of 1973, after the local government reorganization, were anxious to divorce themselves from the legacy of the past. They wanted to start afresh and show themselves to be whiter than white. Unfortunately, their efforts were often opposed by the Liberals for historical reasons rather than objective ones. During those first four years the Labour Group clearly saw that I was not going to oppose for the sake of opposing. If I thought the group policy on

Education or Social Services was right, I would support it. The council was trying to do a sound job in these fields with a prudent eye on a diminishing budget. Durham County Council never espoused dubious or contentious causes as occasionally did some of the London boroughs. Consequently, I was able to support them on most occasions without the slightest qualms of conscience. A humorous anecdote might illustrate this. Councillor Joe Gordon, an old and experienced Socialist councillor, once said to me, 'Father, you were paid a great compliment in the group meeting yesterday' - the group was a private meeting of Labour councillors held prior to any important Education or Policy decision, when they would thrash things out, and would try to arrive at a consensus. Joe went on, 'The leader, Councillor George Fishburn, was getting rather angry about the Liberals and the opposition in general.' He had thumped the table and blurted out 'I divent care what any of you say . . . Caden's the only "fairly bugger" among the lot of them! That was indeed high praise from George Fishburn, Father,' said Joe. Probably, Joe was right.

COMMUNITY HEALTH COUNCILS

During my first session on the county council I had gained sufficient confidence among my Socialist colleagues for them to appoint me to be their representative on Sunderland Community Health Council. There were still many patients in Winterton Hospital from the Sunderland area, hence the representative link with Durham. Remember, I had spent nine happy years working in the Sunderland Health Scene in the 1950s so I knew it like the back of my hand. Moreover, many people in that area still knew *me* in 1975! Within twelve months I had been elected Chairman of the Community Health Council, with its dynamic young Chief Executive or Secretary called Drew Kimber. Community health councils were the watchdogs of the NHS. Their members were drawn from elected councils, voluntary organizations and the medical and nursing professions. They were supposed to represent the customer's interest in the NHS, and were to monitor its every aspect and ensure that the public got value for money in the delivery of health care. Drew was a very knowledgeable secretary and he had excellent contacts with the media, especially with people like John Bailey, the very experienced features writer of the *Sunderland Echo*. It was very high profile as CHCs went. With my own very long experience of patients and their needs through my NHS chaplaincies, I was soon able to forge sound and constructive links with the Health Authority itself, and with the Ambulance Service.

After three years Drew left us for another post in the NHS. The Conservative Government at the time had reservations as to whether they would get rid of CHCs altogether so Drew's Chief Executive post was 'frozen'. The Regional Health Authority asked me as Chairman, if I could keep the CHC afloat for a short time by acting as Chief Executive as well as Chairman! I had full-time secretarial help in the office and I agreed to do this. Chairman and members of CHCs were unpaid but were entitled to travel expenses. However, instead of the couple of months fill-in time that was envisaged, the moratorium eventually stretched out into eighteen months! This meant that I had to drive through to CHC Headquarters in Frederick Street, Sunderland three afternoons a week and ensure that every aspect of Drew's job was carried out. I had just appointed a new Personal Secretary to Drew around the time of his departure. She *had* been Belsie Gallagher and a very popular schoolgirl in St Mary's School during my curate days in Sunderland! Belsie Wilson was a very efficient secretary who knew the Health Service very well and soon she was able to lessen the frequency of my visits to Frederick Street. I was delighted to learn that some years later, after I had progressed to be Vice-Chairman of South West Durham Health Authority, she, in turn, was promoted to the job of Chief Executive or Secretary and did it exceptionally well. I was to meet her in her retirement year as we were leaving King's Cross on the same train. We spent a wonderful 2½-hour journey recalling our NHS experiences and our forty-odd-year friendship!

SOUTH-WEST DURHAM HEALTH AUTHORITY

At the end of six years as Chairman of Sunderland Community Health

Council the Government decided on yet another reorganization of the NHS. About 1980 they set up new District Health Authorities. These Health Authorities would have about fifteen members, comprised of NHS consultants, elected members and members of voluntary organizations with other nursing and medical professional input. The Chairman would be directly appointed by the Secretary of State. George Chetwynd, the former Stockton MP and the then Chairman of the Northern Regional Health Authority, had asked me if I would be prepared to transfer from the CHC Chairmanship to be Chairman of one of the new Health Authorities, either in Durham or Sunderland. Membership of Health Authorities automatically excluded membership of a CHC and vice versa. He suggested that the £15,000 emolument could go to charity! In the event, when the chairmanships were announced, a new Health Authority based at Northallerton was given a Brother of St John of God Hospital as its Chairman. George very apologetically told me that it would look bad if two of the new chairmen in the Northern Region turned out to be Catholic reverends! The new Health Authorities would have a CHC dimension built into them. They would contain many appointees who had CHC experience. This was why the Government delayed for eighteen months trying to decide whether they could disband CHCs altogether.

In due course I was elected Vice-Chairman of the South-West Durham Health Authority which included both Winterton Hospital and Bishop Auckland General Hospital. The Chairman I worked with during my ten years as Vice-Chairman was Erica Wallace. Erica became a very efficient chairperson and she got to know her patch extremely well. She would rely on me to keep a special eye on Winterton which contained the bulk of the beds in the Authority. Since I was working there as RC Chaplain from 1966 I knew the hospital and the staff extremely well. She would also rely on me for any liaison or lobbying with the rest of the members - they had elected me as Vice-Chairman for the life of the Health Authority. We were fortunate to have a strong clinical input from the various consultants who were active members of the Authority, as well as a political dimension, from other members. Those ten years in the 1980s were happy ones and, I think, fruitful years. The Health Service, in my opinion, during those years was actively involved in streamlining itself. It succeeded in cutting budget costs without too seriously affecting its own efficacy, and without noticeably being detrimental to the patient.

Between 1980 and 1990 the Chief Executive was still, in practice, responsible and answerable to the Chairman and Authority members. However, after 1990, when the Health Service Trusts emerged on a massive scale, the non-executive membership of the Health Authorities was suddenly reduced by about two-thirds, to five members, and their power was emasculated. The greatly diminished number of members became very much indeed 'non-executive'! In contrast the Chief Executive's powers were suddenly multiplied! Efficiency bonuses were often available to those of them who could achieve a particular timescale in any programme. Some of the new Chief Executives were business managers; often they had no medical or nursing experience whatsoever, and they managed the NHS as a business. Their own salaries increased out of all proportion to the former Health Service salaries. They had been appointed by a government that was by now letting ideology outpace empathy and care of the patient. Moreover, the new non-executive members who should have been safeguarding the interests of the consumer were in most cases political appointees and they were also paid. There were many Mental Health Trusts, especially in the South of England, which moved with quite unseemly haste to empty the old-style psychiatric and mental handicap hospitals. They pushed patients out into the community under the veil of Care in the Community when they knew only too well that the care was not actually there! It was only the pressure of the bad publicity connected with some of these cases that forced, first Virginia Bottomly, and later Stephen Dorrell, to slow the whole mad gallop down to a canter.

Thank goodness that the hospital I knew and worked for for thirty years, Winterton Hospital, was never guilty of these abuses. The rehabilitation in the community of all patients, so far, has taken place in a careful and well-planned manner, having regard to the dignity and happiness of the patient. Peter Brotherhood, the Chief Executive of the 1980s and his assistant Colin Gatiss, helped by people like Val Suddes, laid a good foundation for this rehabilitation programme. Len Wilson, the Chief Executive of the 1990s and his assistant, Eleanor Lane, continued the decanting process in a sensitive and humane way. But then they both had long experience in the Health Service and in this very field of psychiatry.

My active involvement in the administration came to an abrupt end in 1990. With the advent of the Trusts and the extra powers for Chief Executives, the Government didn't want people like me around. We had spent a lifetime working in a voluntary capacity trying to make the lives of hospital patients happier and more fulfilled - *we* would be an obstacle to speedy progress! Consequently, many of the old Authority members of the 1980s disappeared from the scene. The pretexts of this disappearance were varied and specious, perhaps age or perhaps even an availability for appointment as non-executive members to the Trusts; but the underlying reason would be the same: we had the wrong philosophy of care! Sadly this meant that one was often perceived as the wrong political shade, since the bulk of the ensuing appointments would be 'political'. This was unlike the bulk of the appointments made to the 1980 Health Authorities which were genuinely made on ability and proven voluntary expertise in the Health Service.

CHAPTER XXVI

A HAPPY REUNION

Remember Bebe on the *Mauretania* in 1950? She had come to Europe to spend her third college year with her Rosary College friends at Fribourg University. At the end of that year they were to visit the British Isles. By this time I was working at St Mary's in Sunderland. Father Dan gave me twenty-four hours off to renew acquaintance with Bebe who was to stay for a few days with my family in Middlesbrough. It was great to see her again. My sister, Pauline, who was the first in the family to learn to drive a car, took us down to Scarborough. The day was very enjoyable, although somewhat marred by the usual showers and north-easterly wind. When I went back to my parish in Sunderland that night, Bebe linked up with her Rosary friends in Edinburgh. The group had travelled from Dublin to Edinburgh while Bebe had come to stay with my family in Middlesbrough. She wanted at least to see Princes Street, before returning to Chicago. Their itinerary from Edinburgh to London was to include a break at York to see York Minister. I had arranged to wave them off at York on the final lap of their journey back to America. My father, who had a railway pass on which I could travel and loved to ride on trains when he was not working, accompanied me to York.

It's hard to believe when I look back, but a formal handshake was our final goodbye in the corridor of that train! In 1951 the conditioning of thirteen years seminary training was still very much in evidence. Even warmth, let alone emotion or an embrace, were definitely not par for the course.

It would be fifteen years before I would meet Bebe again. Regular Christmas cards and occasional letters would cherish and deepen our friendship. The idea of joining her teachers as a nun at Rosary College soon faded. She fell in love with a certain Joseph O. Nicolau, a close friend of her brother, Buddy, who was in the American forces at that time. In due course they married and over the next six years had four children. Bebe sent me photographs of the children as they came along, with frequent, urgent invitations to come out to Chicago and stay with them. She never actually sent me a photo of this Joseph O. Nicolau, consequently I could only conjure up an imaginary picture of him . . . a picture which was eventually to prove utterly removed from reality. They planned to come to Europe, minus the children, for their tenth wedding anniversary - eventually they made it for their fourteenth!

Joe Nicolau, as I was to find out later, was not the greatest tourist in the world, no more than myself. After being 'run ragged in Italy' where Bebe's father had been born, Joe was looking forward to a quiet few days in London, prior to flying back to Chicago. Bebe had written earlier to tell me that they would contact me from Italy about the details of their four-day stay in London. She was not aware that postcards from Italy have a habit of arriving in England after one's return! She sent me a card from Rome with the details of their London visit. The trouble was that I did not receive this card in Dipton until the Friday of the weekend of their arrival in London! Consequently I was not at the Kensington Palace Hotel to meet them - indeed, I had no hope of getting down to London at all that weekend! It was the busiest weekend of our St Patrick's parish year when we held the annual garden fête. I telephoned my sister Mary and husband Jim Kennedy to ask them could they deputize for me at the Kensington Palace Hotel and show the Nicolaus London. Jim had worked in the City for years and he knew London better than many a taxi driver! Moreover, Mary knew Bebe well - she had stayed with the Romano family in 1952 when she had spent a year in America on teaching exchange. Joe and Bebe were delighted to meet up with Jim and Mary, but on the Friday night when Bebe telephoned St Patrick's it would have been obvious to a deaf man that she was less than pleased with me! Father Duffy rushed from the presbytery to the confessional where I was doing my Friday night stint, and shouted to me that there was some 'excitable woman' on the phone who sounded American. 'Where are you?' the voice began. 'Why aren't you here? Didn't you get my card?' the voice continued with just a touch of hysteria. When I finally got through to Bebe that the card had only arrived that morning, and that I would only be able to come to London early on Monday morning, that was the last straw! Monday would be no good - they were flying back to Chicago at 1 p.m. on Monday. Her voice betrayed dismay, almost rejection - I felt terrible! Priests in the affluent Chicago suburbs in the early 1960s had a much more relaxed lifestyle than their English counterparts. She finally told me curtly that she would get back to me. On the Saturday night I received another phone call. She would fly up to Newcastle on Sunday morning and I had better be there at Newcastle Airport to meet the plane at noon! She would have four hours with me and then would return at 5 p.m. - the only other plane back to Heathrow that day.

Through the intercession of housekeeper, Hilda, I had persuaded Father Duffy to say the eleven o'clock Mass instead of his very abbreviated eight-o'clock Mass. There was no question of entertaining in the presbytery - very few presbyteries in the 1950s were actually 'Home' to the curate! I arranged to take her to my good friends, Bibby and Bryn Thomas, who had a lovely bungalow in Whickham. It was only about ten minutes from the airport itself. Bebe had told me on the phone that she would be alone as Joe intended to have a look at Madame Tussauds. I was later to learn that Joe had told Bebe she was quite crazy to fly to Newcastle. 'Bebe', he said, 'you've done lots of crazy things in the fourteen years we've been married . . . but you can't be serious . . . you mean to say that you are going to fly four hundred miles to see a priest for a few hours who you only met once in your life when you were a college girl?'

Bebe, on the verge of tears, simply said, 'I've got to do it, Joe.'

Later on Joe told the story with considerable embellishment. 'I admit, Father, I gave her a very hard time . . . I had heard about "Father John" throughout most of my marriage, until I was tired of hearing the name. When you weren't at the Kensington Palace Hotel I told her that priests meet a lot of people in fifteen years. If he had really wanted to come he would have been down here to meet us. However, I could see she was determined to go and I said I would get her a flight, but I would not go - I wanted to see Madam Tussauds.'

It was one of the hottest May days I had known. I drove up to Newcastle airport and parked near the perimeter fence - yes, perimeter fence. Newcastle airport was not an international airport in 1966. There were no customs or real terminal buildings. It was possible to walk onto the airfield. It was so hot I slipped off my jacket and my large, plastic Roman collar, and left them in the car. The thought did cross my mind also that I would be rather more incognito without them. I was realist enough to know that our reunion after fifteen years might involve more than the formal handshake of York station at our last farewell in 1951! I was worried that some Catholic on the airfield might recognize me and be disedified by what they saw. Yes! Forty years ago priests had to be so careful that they did not disedify members of their flock or people outside it.

The four-engined Britannia rolled down the runway and came to a stop. After a few people had descended from the high landing steps, Bebe suddenly appeared outside the door of the plane. She spotted me on the tarmac and waved excitedly to me as she saw me walking forward. She hurried down the steps off the plane and, since she had told me she would be alone, I never bothered to look at anybody else behind her. I glanced around rather furtively to make sure that nobody on the grass verge was known to me, and I moved forward as she ran towards me and we met in a flurry of hugs and kisses. As Bebe hugged me with tears of joy, I suddenly noticed a large, powerful, handsome, dark man with a movie camera apparently pointing in our direction who had appeared from nowhere. Immediately I thought there must be some celebrity on the plane who was already behind me. In complete panic I thought it must be Tyne Tees Television - I would be on the six o'clock news, affectionately hugging a petite, dark, beautiful woman! The bishop would surely see it. Frantically, I looked back over my shoulder to spot the celebrity, but there was nobody in sight. Belatedly I turned Bebe in her tracks to avoid the camera's gaze, but, to my horror, the movie cameraman merely moved over to his right and continued filming! There could be no doubt about it now, he *was* filming us! My heart sank. Just at that moment he slipped the camera round his waist so that it was now hanging at his back, suddenly smiled a huge smile and bounded towards us. He grabbed both of us in a huge bear-hug. 'Father John,' he said. It was my introduction to Joseph O. Nicolau!

The three hours in Bibby's Whickham bungalow and the lunch in the garden went only too quickly. Joe, who is one of the best and funniest story-tellers I have ever met, had us nearly ill with laughter on that sunny lawn. He confided, 'I had heard about this Father John only too regularly for the last fourteen years. I was convinced that maybe he did not remember the *Mauretania* quite as vividly as Bebe did. Why had he not been down to meet us at the Kensington Palace? So when I was actually booking Bebe's ticket, I thought I must just see this guy. Anyway I really *should* accompany my wife. My curiosity was beginning to get the better of me. Here was my chance to see if this priest was for real. Much to Bebe's joy I got *two* tickets instead of one. Father John was expecting Bebe alone. I had the movie camera so I would operate independently. I would capture their reunion on film for posterity and be able to show it to the children when we got back to Chicago.' Before Bryn and Bibby drove the Nicolaus back to the airport, they made me promise solemnly that I would come out to Chicago the next year. I promised them, bid them a now happier farewel1 and returned back to Dipton to do the Benediction at 6 p.m.!

MY FIRST TRANSATLANTIC FLIGHT

A few weeks after this happy reunion I was appointed to Sedgefield as Parish Priest. As I have indicated, I spent the next eighteen months running round in circles trying to cope with the full-time hospital chaplaincies, working fifteen-hour days, and knowing that in practice I was completely isolated in my apostolate. My nearest priest neighbours at Ferryhill and Trimdon were both semi-invalids themselves, and so I never sought any relief from them. This meant that I had to look to Stockton or Billingham for any help. Remember, there were no hospital bleeps in those days. If a Stockton priest offered to cover for me, he had to be prepared to remain near his phone. They would tell me, 'If you ever want a day off, Jack, just give me a ring.' However, on the two or three occasions I contacted them they were sorry, they could not do it that day. Any other day, OK! I decided it was simpler just to get on with it. However, there was one exception, Father Ossie Clement. Ossie was a saintly parish priest at St Bede's, Stockton, who always took great delight in being of service. During the twenty years from 1971 to 1991 when I was called upon to help with the training of deacons by Ushaw, I would use Ossie as a role model for them - a role model in removing barriers when initially answering the telephone. At any time of the day or night Ossie would pick up his phone and say in a warm, friendly voice, 'Stockton 76164, Father Clement at your service.' How important it is for us priests to make callers on the telephone feel that they are glad they phoned.

Yes, I was so busy I never bothered about a regular day off. In any case, I had my mother living with me so I didn't need to drive twenty miles to visit her. To get away for holiday I needed to persuade a supply priest to come and live in my presbytery while I was away. My promise to Joe and Bebe to visit Chicago in the summer of 1967 could not be fulfilled. However, I was determined to make it there the next summer. My old boyhood friend, Father Owen Murray, who was working as a missionary in Pakistan, would be home for a few months - he would be happy to come and live for a month in my house in Sedgefield. My mother and Vera would look after him. My mother, of course, had known him since he had been a schoolboy at St Cuthbert's School, Hartlepool with me; she had also been very friendly with Owen's parents who were both now dead.

My first trip to America was indeed memorable. I went on a chartered flight from Prestwick Airport to New York and the plane was a four-engined prop-jet known as the Britannia. English airlines were just then acquiring their first Boeing 707s, but these were not yet available for the cheaper charter flights. The Britannia was a very reliable aircraft that could carry 150 passengers. Its range was about sufficient to get it safely across the Atlantic on its twelve-hour flight. To say I was somewhat apprehensive is an understatement. However, I had to appear to be cool, because most of the charter club were Catholics and they were obviously encouraged by the presence of a youngish priest in their midst. If they had only known how I myself felt inside!

We had been in the air about ten hours when the captain's voice came through on the intercom and informed us that Kennedy Airport was fog-bound - we would have to divert to Boston. He warned us that he would have to conserve fuel, and would be mainly flying on two engines at a time, but it would be perfectly safe. Almost an hour later he told us that we would be landing at Logan Airport, Boston in twenty minutes or so. He said, 'We will have to save fuel and will make a very steep descent in the last few minutes, so please don't panic - I know the capabilities of my aeroplane.' Outside the aircraft windows, there was just thick, white fog visible. We began this steep dive and it seemed to go on for ever! I was fervently saying my prayers. I could see the headlines in the *Northern Echo*: 'Priest perishes in plane nose dive'. After what seemed an eternity, the cloud suddenly disappeared and we were in bright sunshine. As we continued to dive I could see the sunshine glittering on the water of the bay which half surrounds Boston Airport. I was sure the captain would not be able to pull out of the dive and we would go straight into the water. At the last moment he managed to flatten out the plane, and we skimmed over the water to the adjacent runway to make a perfect landing. There was huge, heartfelt applause from nearly everyone on the aircraft! While they waited for news that the fog had lifted at Kennedy, we were allowed into the terminal to get refreshment. When we learned that we would not continue to New York for at least another hour and a half, I made a quick decision. I was quite sure that the captain had used several of his 'lives' in managing to land at Boston at all! Even after refuelling it would still be another three hours or more before we were off the plane at Kennedy Airport, and then I would have to get another plane to Chicago on United Airlines. I thought that the United Airlines office in the airport might be prepared to change my ticket so that I could fly from Boston to Chicago instead of from Kennedy to Chicago in three hours' time. To my relief they agreed to change my ticket and within half an hour I was luxuriating in a real jet - a half-full 727 and my 'Visit USA' ticket took me into the Business Class part of the plane. There seemed to be yards of room compared with my cramped prop-jet Britannia. As I attacked a tasty lobster salad helped down with chilled Chablis, I gazed out of the plane window picking out the clear detail of the terrain five miles below. I think it was at that moment that I began to lose my fear of flying. Thank God that in the 100,000 miles of flying that I would do in the next thirty years this relaxation would continue to be present!

THE CHICAGO WELCOME

I had telephoned the Nicolaus from Boston and told them that I would be arriving at O'Hare on the Boston plane and not the New York plane. O'Hare was supposed to be the busiest airport in the world, with take-offs or landings every thirty seconds! After a tumultuous welcome from Bebe, Joe and the children at the airport I was whisked away to their home in Park Ridge, a suburb about ten minutes' drive from the airport. As Joe's black Cadillac sped smoothly along the eight-lane freeway in the early afternoon, I was flabbergasted by the huge flow of traffic which at the same time was so orderly. Joe had built a special 'pad' for me in 1504, South Crescent, where I would have complete privacy if and when I needed it, with my own bathroom, TV etc. Henceforth, it would be known as 'Father John's Pad'. I had to choke back tears of joy and humility at the love and the sincerity of this welcome!

Park Ridge was a typical Chicago suburb, with its spacious homes and manicured lawns. It had a huge Catholic population and to see the crowds at Our Lady Seat of Wisdom at every Mass in 1968 was an unbelievable experience for me as a priest. When we had started our Sunday evening Mass at St Mary's, Sunderland, in the 1950s we used to pack the church with a thousand people, but that was just *one* Mass. Here in Park Ridge, the church was crowded with a thousand people for *every* Mass on Sunday! Over the next quarter of a century I would say Mass there scores of times. The Nicolau children, Joey, Michelle, Johnny (named after me) and Mary loved to have me leading their Sunday Mass. I was their own 'Father John'! They used to be quite 'slain' with my accent. I never thought that I had a 'frightfully, frightfully' accent, but Michelle, particularly, loved to hear it. She would say, 'Pardon me, Father,' and pretend she hadn't heard properly what I had said, just to get me to repeat something. It was only when she would 'fold up' with laughter that I eventually saw that she was taking the mickey. Then I would really put on a real Oxford accent to complete her amusement. In my early years of preaching in America, I used to attempt a hybrid drawl which at least assured me that people understood me. Later on, however, I would adopt the 'Richard Burton' approach with its clipped tone clarity and resonance. I think it was much more popular with Americans, just as we English find an American accent a change from time to time.

Joe Nicolau was never too keen on eating out, or barbecues in the garden – the backyard as the Americans so humbly call it. For starters, the mosquitoes were an enemy to be reckoned with. Joe, however, believed that the 'backyard' was always a licence to entertain, as far as Bebe was concerned. She would start off by inviting six people to dinner. However, because they had a huge backyard, Bebe's generous spirit and 'love of her neighbour' would, within forty-eight hours have multiplied that half-dozen to twenty-four going on thirty-six! The original, select dinner party group would have lost any identity it originally had and very soon the numbers dictated that the cosy dinner party simply had to become an outdoor event. Bebe's brother, Buddy, and his wife, Florence, had seven children; her brother, Michael, and wife, Mitzi, had three children; there were also half a dozen Park Ridge Catholic families living within two or three minutes of the Nicolaus. Hadn't they all heard about this English priest 'Father John'? Bebe was not prepared to keep them waiting!

There resulted, therefore, quite early in my Park Ridge stay what was the most wonderful, fairytale party which one could possibly imagine. The ten Rosary College girls of the *Mauretania* of 1950, like Bebe, had married and got on with their lives in various parts of the United States! Bebe invited them to come to a *Mauretania* Reunion Party where they would meet up once again with the chaplain-cum-chaperone of the 1950 Atlantic crossing. Their numbers were bolstered by other members of the Nicolau and Romano families and Park Ridge friends. However, the guests of honour were the 'Rosary Class of 1950' who flew in or drove in from various parts of the United States, some three, four or five children later! Dorothy Tully, one of the 1950 group, lived only a half-hour's drive from the Nicolaus and she helped with the logistics of the get-together; Joe masterminded the huge cooking operation, under his wife's direction; the backyard was duly festooned and lanterned; the full resources of Moran Brothers, the large liquor firm founded by Bebe's father, and now run by her brothers, were made readily available. There ensued a party to make all parties pale into insignificance and I still get a lump in my throat when I think of that night! Very humbly I think of the fantastic thoughtfulness and love of this couple and their children for me. How often during the following thirty years we would come together for a baptism or a wedding or simply a holiday. How often I would share in the joys and sorrows of their intimate friends, who in turn would become my friends - people like Dr Luke and Marie Gremelli. Other friends I would make while holidaying with them in Long Beach or on the shores of Lake Michigan, like Joe and Lorraine O'Rourke, and through them, Veronica Wunder, whom I would later meet on a 'blind tennis date'. The Nicolaus became 'family' to me. I often think of my Boston Catholic Steward on the *Mauretania*. I did not want to disedify him, and so I somewhat reluctantly accepted the place he had reserved for me next to the *two nuns*, never knowing that the row of empty chaise-longues next to them belonged to Bebe, Lolly, Dedy, Dorothy and the others of the Class of '50. As I stated in an earlier chapter, that reluctant act of resignation on my part changed the whole course of my social life as a priest!

I MEET DR LUKE

I had been frequently regaled by the Nicolaus with stories of this Dr Luke Gremelli, an eminent Chicago physician who had taken on the spiritual charisma of his namesake St Luke. He attended Mass every day before he began work in his hospital. Certainly, according to Bebe, he was on a shortlist for 'canonization'! After a week or so in Park Ridge I was to meet him and it happened like this.

I had been at the Ridge Moor Country Club all day with Dr Luke's wife, Marie, Bebe and half a dozen children! Ridge Moor was a typical Country Club, with golf course, tennis courts, magnificent swimming pool and hotel-like clubhouse. I discovered later that no money ever actually changed hands in that club. Everything was debited to the member's number! In the meantime I was getting a little embarrassed that I couldn't even buy anyone a drink or a sandwich. On this particular day, in a fit of stubbornness, I steadfastly refused to have any food or anything to drink during the long '80-degree day' by the pool. We were scheduled to go back to Dr Luke's house to meet him when he arrived back from his work at the hospital. I had not eaten anything all day, nor had I drunk even a 7-Up or a Coke. When Marie, Luke's wife, arrived with me at her beautiful home, she insisted that I would mark the occasion with a martini. To me a 'martini' was a measure of vermouth bianco with plenty of ice and tonic. Marie's martinis, I later learned, were quite notorious! They consisted of a huge measure of gin, with a small dash of vermouth and lemon, with some added sparkle from a touch of tonic. I had a huge thirst - no liquid all day in that damp heat, so I downed it very quickly to quench my thirst and Marie replenished my glass immediately before going back to the kitchen with Bebe. When I was halfway through the second martini, I felt a warm feeling behind my eyes. I heard Marie telling Bebe in the kitchen that Luke would be here any minute. I tried to move along the couch a little and to my horror found that I couldn't feel my legs at all! As I struggled to lift them, I suddenly felt the room moving crazily around in ever-widening circles. What a fool I have been, I thought, to go all day without food or drink! I found that if I kept perfectly still, my head could cope with the circling movement of the room - in a few moments this subject for canonization would be home and he would be looking forward to meeting this Father John from England. I was absolutely mortified at the thought. I knew that I must not even attempt to get up, whatever happened. I heard Marie greeting him as he came through the connecting door from the garage. He bowled in all smiles, and shouted across the room, 'Don't get up, Father.' He moved quickly across the last two yards in front of the couch and reached out to shake my hand and welcome me to his home. 'I see Marie has been mixing you one of her martinis, Father . . .' He had obviously noticed immediately my glazed look as soon as he came into the room! He called out to Marie and ordered some strong black coffee so that during the next hour I gradually got my feet back. It was the first and also the last occasion in my life when I would be intoxicated.

CHAPTER XXVII

THE LATE SEVENTIES

My work in the parish went on very much as usual. The hospitals continued to be a very demanding, but at the same time, a very rewarding ministry. During my first eight years in Sedgefield, the District General Hospital continued to demand most of my working day and night. I had trained the nursing staff to call the priest when any Catholic patient was in any danger at all, or when the patient or the relatives would ask for the priest. This meant that my priest colleagues in Stockton, Thornaby, Billingham, or Trimdon and Ferryhill would confidently leave it to me to give the Blessing of the Sick, and do the necessary follow-up with Holy Communion for any of their parishioners who would be admitted to Sedgefield General or its coronary care unit. I have stated already that in the 1970s, the concept of the last rites was gradually being debunked altogether and the emphasis was on helping the patient to get better. Since I was on call twenty-four hours a day, my colleagues didn't even have to worry, and usually didn't. Indeed, the only priest who always seemed to know if any of his flock had been hospitalized was a very elderly priest in Norton, Father Robert Thornton, known to the diocesan priests as 'The Reev'. As a young curate in St Joseph's, Hartlepool, around 1927, 'The Reev' used to keep the four-year-old Caden entertained when he would visit my parents' first home in Carlton Street. He used to draw engines and trains for the rather demanding youngster. He had been a convert himself and would often ring me in Sedgefield to ask me 'to give a blessing to so-and-so - not a Catholic, John, but a very good man'. 'The Reev' was certainly one of the early ecumenists!

In order to lessen the number of night calls for Sedgefield General, I developed a system that probably ensured for me a few more restful nights than I would otherwise have enjoyed. In the sixteen wards there were always patients who were dying or who were dangerously ill. I made a habit of calling into the hospital every night between 10-11 p.m. to visit and pray with the dying. I would also check at the same time that no new patients had come into the acute medical wards or the CCU during the afternoon or early evening. If I found new patients, then I would give them the short form of the Blessing of the Sick straight away and make a note of this in the case notes folder. This meant that any night nurse would know immediately that the priest had attended the sick person.

However, despite all my efforts, I was still frequently talking to Night Sister Elsie Fraser between midnight and 7 a.m. Sedgefield was nearly always on 'bed bureau' because its sister hospital in Stockton was much smaller and always full. Frequently, patients would be admitted to Sedgefield during the night and Elsie would telephone me. She was quite convinced that I didn't go to bed at all, and claimed that I always answered the phone on the second or third ring. However, I was a light sleeper and conditioned to reach out and grab my bedside phone immediately. Fortunately, if I pulled on my clothes over my pyjamas, I could be speeding up to the hospital within minutes. I could be up and back again in bed within the hour. One of the bonuses of Sedgefield parish for me, on the hundreds of occasions when I returned from the hospital in the early hours of the morning, was to see the dim shape of the cattle or sheep in the 'Showfield' outside my bedroom window, when I would hear the comforting sound of their dialogue. It was never like this in the back streets of Sunderland St Mary's, when I came back during the night from the Royal Infirmary!

In addition to the parish and the hospitals, I now had my work and responsibilities with the Town Council and the County Council. In spite of being territorially large, my parish was small by diocesan standards - only about 150 families. Naturally, my first priority was to the parishioners. I knew them all and I visited all their homes at least annually. I had a very active St Vincent de Paul Society, which did excellent work in Winterton Hospital by organizing fortnightly 'Club Nights' for the patients. Three of its early members, John Forsyth, Peter Cullen and Jim Amlin, are still there after thirty years. Peter Ebblewhite, a lifelong member from Trimdon, joined us later and is still with us. We have also recruited others from time to time. Another of the Parish groups that gave me some sense of achievement over the years was 'The Family Circles'. I would encourage groups of couples to meet together socially about every five or six weeks, and they would meet in turn in one or other of their homes. Tea or coffee and biscuits was the only permitted refreshments. I would go to the home of the host couple for that night and would encourage them to make their own agenda. There would often ensue a spirited and free-ranging discussion about ethics or religion, which helped them to cope better with the demands of a materialistic world. Their regular get-togethers also deepened social bonds and friendships and these in turn gave the parish a feeling of real identity. Tim and Anne Jeanes were founder members of the initial circle - they were still around to become honorary members of the third group I would launch twenty-five years later!

BILL NEVENS

In my first ten years at St John Fisher we had a wonderful social dimension in the parish. I was intent on raising funds for a new primary school of our own. I organized very frequent social evenings at the Fishburn Working Men's Club. Apart from raising an extra £1,000 a year - a lot of money in the seventies - it also highlighted the Catholic Church as the springboard for social life in the Sedgefield area community. Our Fishburn social evenings and the St Patrick's Night dances were always sell-outs. From 1967 I had the help of a wonderful right-hand man whose name was Bill Nevens. Bill was a local confectionery manager and was a natural organizer. He could provide us with a talented professional organist, a drummer and a first-class cabaret act every time. Meanwhile, the parish ladies, marshalled by Connie Nicholson and the wives of the SVP brothers, would spend the afternoons of the Fishburn social nights preparing refreshments for the socials. From being one of the poorer diocesan parishes in 1966, these social events helped us to establish a very sound financial base over the next fifteen years. Indeed, this base has held us in good stead right up to the present day.

VERA

However, through all these developments, and through my regular fifteen-hour working days during my first twenty years at Sedgefield, with their huge variety, one person especially enabled me to spread myself so widely - my housekeeper, Vera.

Vera had been prompted and encouraged by my mother to begin to believe in herself. She had multifarious talents: she was a fine cook, a female Percy Thrower, a good decorator, an excellent businesswoman-cum-bookkeeper; she loved to run raffles and Christmas card stalls and piety stalls - it was a continuation of her earlier life, helping to run Co-op branches at Leadgate and confectionery departments at Newcastle's Fenwicks. For most of the first eleven years, my mother 'Gert' was a prominent member of the St John Fisher household. Gert herself certainly never lacked self-confidence and generally persuaded Vera how to manage me! Very often, hospital emergencies would delay me and lunch would have to be warmed up or might even be spoilt. Gert gave Vera a very practical guide for avoiding frustration and tests of temperament at lunchtimes. 'Have the table set, Vera,' she would tell her, 'and then tell him the lunch will be on the table soon; just relax for a few minutes with the *Northern Echo*.' It worked, as did other pieces of advice that Gert would impart to Vera. No wonder that my

Vera and the Author at work in the Church

friend Father George (Dolan) described me, tongue-in-cheek, to some of my classmates as 'happy but henpecked'. Incidentally, my mother developed something of an aberration in her later years in Sedgefield. She discovered a previously unknown love of 'the gee-gees'.

GERT AND THE HORSES

I had a classmate - Father Frank McLoughlin - who worked in Manchester. 'Titch' as he was known to his Ushaw friends and to us in Sedgefield, loved the races. One day he came to Sedgefield for race day. He had a good tip from a racehorse owner friend for Chepstow that day and Vera was dispatched to Ron Mann's betting shop to put on the bet. Gert, who had never bet on a horse in her life, was persuaded by Father Titch to have a half-crown on the horse. It won at 10-l and Gert was absolutely thrilled. That night, before he left for Manchester, Titch gave her another tip for the next day - and this one came in at 8-1. It was all just too much for my mother - she was hooked!

Vera's father had been a great betting man and so Vera knew all the trainers and jockeys through listening to her father. Her expertise was enlisted by Gert and together they studied form on an almost daily basis. Eventually, I suggested to Gert that she should phone in her bet. Parishioners would think that I was the one that was laying the bets when they saw Vera slipping into the betting shop on an almost daily basis. Gert and Vera would have a morning consultation with the help of the *Northern Echo* and the *Daily Express*. Later, she would look intently at the horses in the paddock and if she liked the look of two or three in the same race, she would phone Ron and say, 'Do me Blue Peter, Ron, and also so-and-so.' Ron was always very patient with my mother, considering that her bet would never be more than 'two bob' at a time. The betting interest was always a barometer for Gert's health. If she had been poorly for a few days, we always knew when she felt better for she would suddenly say to Vera, 'Let's have a look at the *Northern Echo*, Darkie' (Gert's nickname for Vera). Ron christened her 'The Reverend Mother' and, I suspect, would heave a gentle sigh of relief when she went to visit my sister in Westcliffe for a few weeks.

His phone would not get too many two-bob bets during that period.

MINISTRY TO PRIESTS

In 1985, Bishop Lindsay asked me, as Vice-Chairman of the Council of Priests, along with five other priests, to form a working group in preparation for the launching in the diocese of 'Ministry to Priests'. Some time before, Father Sam Mullally and Father Goff-Bryce had proposed me as a candidate for the vice-chairmanship of the council and I had been duly elected. However, I never had any opportunity to test my skills, since Bishop Hugh was always present to chair his own council. Maybe he thought I might give too much away. Only towards the end of his episcopate, when his health had deteriorated, did I have any opportunity to put my Community Health Council and District Health Authority Chairmanship experience to the test.

Our sub-committee met half a dozen times over the year. Bishop Hugh, quite rightly, wanted to get it right from the start. Looking back now over twelve years, I'm sure that his caution was justified, and he did get it right. Father Dennis Tindall was appointed as the first coordinator and the Ministry to Priests was launched. I was easily the oldest priest on the working party and indeed, the oldest priest in ministry. My only regret was that we didn't have something like this thirty years before. The support it gave to priests, both in the one-to-one relationships, as well as in the very disparate support groups was tremendous. These support groups were very varied: there were two or three walking groups, a golfing group, a sailing group and a theatre group, to mention but a few.

The basic intention of each group was to get nine or ten priests away together in one of their favourite leisure activities, but to include an overnight stay away from the presbytery in the deal. I volunteered to organize a theatre group and we had some wonderful times together. We tried out all-in packages at the Stephen Joseph Theatre-in-the-Round, Scarborough plus hotel - this theatre was the workshop for Alan Ayckbourne's wonderful comedies. We tried out meal-and-matinee at the RSC Festival at Newcastle; we even tried out an occasional sortie to grand opera and ballet. The theatre was important, but secondary - it was the laughs and the stories that proliferate in any intimate gathering of priests that really made it for us. Our theatre group had a wonderful blend of experience, academia and humour. Bob Spence, Kevin Nicholls, Brian Malia, Tom Cunningham, Paul McDermott with his fund of irreverent anecdotes and Jim O' Keefe were the solid foundation, with slightly less dedicated support from Bill Jacks and Laurence Jones. Later on we recruited new members like Ged Lavender, Ronnie Brown, Joe Plumb and former Anglican priest Chris Jackson. By this time one of our 'rising stars' - Jim O' Keefe - had become President of Ushaw College, so we now had a ready-made, ideal venue for ministry - a good dinner, a good video in place of a theatre and an 'overnight' with plenty of laughs! What a boon Ministry to Priests would have been in the 1950s, when scores of young priests were sometimes struggling with their isolation. Lacordaire, many years ago, had described the priesthood as, 'Being a member of all families . . . yet belonging to none.' How true!

CHAPTER XXVIII

ENTER TONY BLAIR

In 1983, I was in the middle of my membership of Durham County Council. I enjoyed the work, as I have already stated. My committees of Social Services, Education and Youth and Community were very much extensions of my pastoral work as a priest and a community leader in Sedgefield. It was in that same year that we suddenly found ourselves with a new potential MP for Sedgefield. He was a young man, possessed of great charm and charisma, with radical new ideas, whose name was Anthony Linton Blair. He soon became known to most people in the area simply as 'Tony.'

I went up to Trimdon as part of an official 'Welcome to the Constituency' meeting, in my capacity as Durham County Councillor for Sedgefield. My colleague and friend, Councillor 'Mick' Terrans, the Durham County Councillor for Trimdon, was orchestrating the welcome. There were representatives from the town councils and the district councils and many other well-known people present. I had heard that we had a new MP just selected, but I had no idea what he looked like, or what manner of man he was. Mick Terrans had told me he was 'a grand lad', and that he was sure that I would like him. Mick's confidence was well-founded - I was immediately impressed with this smiling, frank and charismatic young man. He was charming and articulate, and when he came to shake hands with me, there was a warmth and a candour in our meeting that laid an immediate foundation for our future friendship.

Remember, that I was one of the few people in that hall who did not actually belong to the Labour Party. It was palpably clear that there were to be no barriers with Tony Blair as, without the remotest trace of hesitation, he said, 'I've heard about you, Father, and have been looking forward to meeting you. My wife is a very devout Catholic and I would like to bring her to Mass at your church this Sunday.' I told him the time of my Sunday morning Mass, and said I looked forward to meeting his wife.

On the Sunday, Tony duly arrived at Mass with Cherie and introduced her to me. After Mass, I invited them up to my presbytery for coffee and we spent an enjoyable half-hour getting to know one another better. Cherie was quiet, without being shy. She told me that Anthony Booth, the scouse son-in-law of Alf Garnett's TV series *Till Death Do Us Part* was her father. I could sense immediately that she was a very committed Catholic and a very humble one. It was only later that I learned that she was a much sought-after and highly acclaimed barrister on the London and even the national circuit. By the time we had finished our coffee and chat, I felt that I had known my new parishioners for years. Finally, it was time to go our separate ways: me, to start my weekly Holy Communion round of the sick and the housebound, Cherie and Tony to go back to John Burton's house for Sunday lunch. John, incidentally, a likeable and shrewd ex-Chairman of Sedgefield District Council had, at the last minute, adopted Tony as their selection for the Trimdon branch of the constituency. Tony had knocked at the Burtons' door on the last night for eligibility, and had stated he was looking for a nomination for the Sedgefield parliamentary seat. John was having an informal branch meeting in the house because the main business that night was the European Cup Final! When Tony eventually was interviewed, to quote John, 'He said all the things that the traditional Labour panel didn't want to hear.' However, he said them with such conviction and candour, that John and his friends were impressed, and they finally decided that they would give him the opportunity. The rest is history! Almost as much a part of history, since I have told the story in scores of interviews, is that as Tony and Cherie left my study that first Sunday and passed out into the hallway, Tony noticed a 'Prince' tennis racket standing in the corner of the hall. 'Does someone play tennis in this house, Father?' he asked. I admitted that I still played a rather geriatric game most Saturday or Sunday afternoons. His eyes lit up,'Oh, I love tennis, Father, and I need to keep fit. I will be up here most weekends, could you manage to slot me in for a game?' I told him that I organized a rather informal kind of club. The club was dependent on my telephoning a couple of doctors, teachers and housewives every Friday night or Saturday morning, but I was delighted to offer him a game any weekend when his constituency business would permit it. The very next Saturday Tony became a member of our ad hoc tennis club and has been part of it ever since.

I had nurtured a court at Sedgefield Community Hospital ever since the days when it had been Sedgefield General Hospital. We had managed to keep the tennis netting surround intact and over the years I had provided new tennis nets on a couple of occasions. My friend, Terry Knaggs, who was a handyman as well as a Coxhoe GP, kept the court marked and up to scratch. Sisters-in-law, Pam and Joyce Valks, were always very keen to play. Darren Young has been with us from graduating and has become an ever-present. He and Pam's son, Joe, made sure that the standard of play remained very high, as they elicited the best from their partners. Former Cup Final referee, George Courtney, was a regular also until he was seduced by the golf course, as were Roger Baker, Dave Bewick and Tony Patterson! In later years, local Sedgefield GP, Jim Larcombe, college principal, Tony Simpson and Susan Rodrigues, and young quantity surveyor, Chris Cant, also helped to keep the club viable. Friend and GP, Keith Beveridge, held a watching brief for my fitness until Newcastle United took more and more of his time as 'Club Doctor'. Our regular days for playing were Saturday and Sunday afternoons, winter and summer. It took either snow or heavy rain to dampen our ardour!

For a number of years we would alternate with playing at Ronnie Dixon-Barker's home in Bishopton, where she and her friend, Joyce Mitchell, liked nothing better than a rather more 'social game'. It was Ronnie who out of the blue in 1990, confided to me that our smiling politician 'could be Prime Minister one day'. Prophetic thinking Ronnie! Many a happy Saturday and Sunday we all spent together. Tony, after a gruelling week in Westminster, simply loved it and we loved having him in our midst. He would chivalrously tell the media that I used to beat him which was not true! The only time I would beat him was when Pam Valks, an outstanding player, or Darren would be partnering me and carry me along. Terry Knaggs and I often had a very earnest singles match during the week. For many years Terry was my GP and I think he thought it was medically 'desirable' that he

Some of the Unofficial Tennis Club

should encourage me to win. As I have told scores of interviewers - the Prime Minister is a very sound tennis player with a good 'top spin'. I also thought I observed far more steel in his game as he made it to the top. It's possible, though, that I am just imagining this.

Since he became Leader of the Party and his children are at school in London, our tennis get-togethers have been restricted to school holidays. Now that he is Prime Minister . . . well, who knows?

Cherie turned out to be an extremely devout and committed Catholic. When Euan was born in 1984, we celebrated the baptism in St John Fisher and had the baptismal party afterwards in the village. We repeated the process with the baptisms of Nicholas and Kathryn. It was on these occasions that I met Tony's father - still, at that time a prominent Conservative, and straightaway I knew where Tony got his effortless charm and charisma! Tony's conversion to deep Christian values had taken place at Oxford University, largely due, I think, to his friendship with Peter Thompson, an Australian Anglican priest and mature student at the time. Peter Thompson and Tony wanted to make the Gospel and its values a radical part of their respective lives. Jumping ahead a little, I think also that the influence of Cherie and the children over the last fourteen years have served only to deepen these Gospel values, both at a personal level and at a family level - he understands exactly what makes his wife and children what they are. In an age of ecumenism, he has become completely comfortable and at ease with these values.

Over the years, the Blair family became a very natural part of the Sunday worship at St John Fisher. Since he has never received Holy Communion in Sedgefield, Tony always took great delight in reading one of the lessons whenever asked to do so. Meanwhile, Cherie, like a dozen other mothers, would busy herself with helping her children, while at the same time trying to do her own praying. When I hear Tony referring to the family as the base for a healthy Christian caring community, I know he speaks from the absolute conviction of his own personal experience with the Blair family.

CHAPTER XXIX

HOLIDAYS

A priest, rather like a doctor, has to exercise a certain amount of caution while on holiday, especially if he happens to be in a group or part of a package holiday! My earlier experience when paying to be a guest of Lunn Poly, or later, Thomsons, was that once my identity was known, then 75 per cent of the people in the hotel gave me a wide berth, or at best, regarded me with almost furtive curiosity. The remainder thought, I have never really talked to a priest or a vicar before – I wonder what he thinks about this. 'This' could be anything remotely to do with religion or ethics. The familiar opening gambit would be 'I know you're on holiday, Father, but . . .' There would then ensue a two-hour, one-sided discussion in the hotel lounge, while the shrieks of laughter from the nearby pool or beach would be a reminder that the other 75 per cent were enjoying the Mediterranean sun. I learnt my lesson the hard way! Nevertheless, most priests would be restricted financially to a package holiday, and caution therefore was important.

In my earlier years, I loved to go to Ireland with my friend, Father George. However, we could not always arrange our prospective holiday times together and came the day when I spread my wings and discovered Italy. My initial 'sortie' there was in late October with my friends, Father Mark and Father Wilf. We started off in Rimini in a delightful, small, family hotel, where, because it was the end of the season, we were completely spoilt by the owners! In Rimini we had a never-to-be-forgotten experience of riding on a bus in the rush hour. Our hotel was a couple of miles down the coast from the city. The bus was a 30-seater and at least one hundred people fought their way onto it. I was pinned against one of the windows with an umbrella in one hand, and a bottle of Aurum Liqueur in the other, powerless to move a muscle. Wedged between my umbrella and the Aurum was a lady commuter going home after her day's work in Rimini. She had a very plentiful head of rather bushy blonde hair, the back of which continually tickled my nose for most of the journey - there was no way I could scratch it. Nobody attempted to get off the bus; somehow even more got on when the bus did stop. I could see our stop looming up but not one of the hundred gave an inch, so we had to proceed another mile before there was a wholesale disembarkation! Wilf, Mark and I finally set off back to our hotel, our light holiday attire completely soaked with perspiration that hot, clammy evening.

Eventually, and regretfully, we left Rimini in a small Fiat hire car to drive down to Rome via Assisi. In those days, prior to the completion of the Autostrada del Sol, it was a breathtaking experience. Rome itself was crowded and the Vatican Council was in full swing. Three thousand bishops and their *periti* or theological advisers and translators from all over the world were there. I quickly discovered the advantages of my very small Fiat in the rush hour helter-skelter around some of the larger squares and piazzas! In the jockeying for position at forty miles per hour, it was just as important to look over your shoulder as to look ahead. We loved our first introduction to St Peter's, the Coliseum and the Vatican Museum. There were, of course, some restrictions: St Peter's had been transformed into a huge council chamber for the Vatican Council. One little worry for us was that our own Bishop Cunningham was one of the three thousand bishops in Rome! It would have been just our luck to come around some street corner and have him staring unbelievingly at the three hot, dishevelled and minimally-dressed members of his diocesan clergy. However, it never happened.

From Rome we drove on to Amalfi and Positano in the extreme south of Italy, in search of the fading summer sun. I can well remember revelling in the warm water near the rocky Amalfi beach, scarcely believing that we had been present that morning at the November All Souls Mass in the rather baroque cathedral-like Amalfi church.

We were so much in love with Italy that we went the following year as well, in 1962, this time to Venice. Two of the St Anthony's Grammar School teachers from Sunderland, Moya Carr and a friend, had already been there for two weeks. They were to book some accommodation for us. Venice was so crowded that August that we finished up in a rambling old guest house on the Venice Lido itself. The cost was £1 per day for bed, breakfast and evening meal! It was possibly the only available accommodation in the whole of the Venice area. The guest house was home also to three or four absolutely charming characters, including a Spanish artist-painter and a secretary from Padua. We had some wonderful dinner discussions that would go on well into the night, despite the unwelcome attention of the mosquitoes! It was here that I discovered a simple, but very effective, anti-mosquito device. It was like a Catherine wheel firework which, when lit, would burn very slowly on a saucer for many hours. The mosquitoes hated the rather pleasant fumes it emitted, but we got used to them and it did the trick for us.

At the time, I thought I would never be unfaithful to Italy - until one year I made my first visit to Spain! It began with a pilgrimage to Lourdes, followed by a trip across the Pyrenees and down to Playa de Aro on the Costa Brava. Playa de Aro was just a small fishing village at the time and we had hired a villa, literally on the edge of the beach itself. Both the pilgrimage and the subsequent two weeks in Spain were quite memorable. We had taken Liz Traynor, the girl who had spent six years as governess with Frankie Vaughan before rounding off her career with the British Ambassador in Kuwait. She was home on a long leave and had asked me if my priest friends would consider allowing her to fill the spare seat in the large Ford car we were using for Lourdes. They were quite happy that she should come and she eventually continued on with us to Playa de Aro. Considering that she was a 'lone woman' in the constant company of five very disparate clerics, she handled the situation with great aplomb, and proved to be a very important asset on the trip. She used her charm and tact to maintain a very high standard of good manners, thoughtfulness and even chivalry among her five celibate companions. I was the father figure of the group and became affectionately known to Liz and the others as 'Oncle Jacques'!

Those days on the Costa Brava seduced me into transferring my allegiance from Italy to 'Espana'. We had a wonderful, elderly Spanish lady attached to the villa as a cook and she would make the most delicious tortilla and paella! My role in all these clergy gatherings inevitably seemed to be that of Martha rather than Mary. I would always be the one to 'produce' the evening meal, on the instructions of our Spanish cook. Perhaps, in my role as Oncle Jacques, this was inevitable, I suppose. My perception is that most older priests tend to be Marys rather than Marthas. They have become accustomed to being looked after, cosseted and often spoilt. Father Leo was the biggest Mary of them all. He would usually disappear with his easel for a painting session and would always reappear when the meal was ready, and it was cocktail and tapas time!

ESTEPONA

After Play de Aro, Leo and I tried Estepona. 'Two weeks for the price of one' had a certain appeal. Leo was not the best budget man in the world, he liked to live for the moment and was inclined to let the future take care of itself. He was usually broke during the latter part of any holiday. We found ourselves in a sprawling Club Mediterranee-type complex with about eight hundred post-graduate age group holidaymakers from every Scandinavian and European city. We made sure from the start that we did not advertise the fact that we were Catholic priests! Leo pretended to be in paediatric work and I was - in my case, quite truthfully, of course - working in psychiatry. My early experience of psychiatrists and psychiatric social workers enabled me to be very comfortable in my role. Leo, however, occasionally had more difficulty, especially considering that most of our fellow guests spoke far better English than we spoke French or German or Swedish! Some charming Swedish and Dutch graduates nearly always seemed to be at our table. The dining room had tables for eight and there were no special places. In order to get the best social mix, people just filled a table at random, and no food was served until the table was full. The speciality of our Swedish friends appeared to be child welfare so they showed a lingering curiosity about Leo's 'vocation'! However, we were in great demand as facilitators for sing-songs and barbeques - Leo's ability with the guitar and our joint considerable repertoire of folk music made us central to much of the home-made entertainment at the Club Playa del Sol. Personally, I simply revelled in the holiday even more, because every sport from tennis and volleyball to sailing and horse riding were laid on as normal amenities. I played a lot of tennis with a German post-graduate student called Heinz. Heinz and his friends became very friendly with Leo and myself - friendly enough to have doubts about our real vocation! At our farewell drinks party, Heinz turned to Leo and said, 'Leo, what is it you were saying that you do?' Leo had to think quickly and remembered he was in 'child care'. Heinz then, with a knowing smile, said, 'That is strange, Leo, because I am thinking all the time that you and John are men of the cloth.' Leo didn't know whether to deny it at the last moment - he stated later that he was sure that he heard a cock crow!

BENIDORM

The year after our trip to Estepona, I could not get away with Father Leo. Instead, I discovered a place called Benidorm on the Costa Blanca, and immediately fell in love with it and have been going there ever since. Being on my own and having to cover hospitals meant that the usual summer holidays were 'out' for me. I could not get supply priests when most other priests were themselves on holiday. Benidorm is a winter resort and so I could be fairly confident of sunshine and a warm sea in October, November, May or June. Moreover, it was possible in those months for me to get supply priests.

My earlier holidays there were taken with my brother-in-law, Jim. Jim worked in the City in shipping and cargo chartering on the Baltic Exchange. His summer holidays were the children's school holidays, but he liked to get away for a week in the autumn or spring. Package holidays to Benidorm from Luton and Gatwick were plentiful and we had some very enjoyable short breaks. My mother thought he would be company for me . . . my sister, Mary thought I would be company for him! Possibly both had a secret agenda. By this time, I had learned the lesson the hard way and always travelled incognito. I am sure that there would be people on our package in the various hotels who would suspect that we might be gay. They would see us constantly together, whether in the dining room or at the bar or elsewhere. Since Benidorm, in the early 1970s, had more than its share of gay bars, it could be a perfectly natural conclusion. If there was a dance or social evening in the hotel, Jim would eventually dispel any such illusion. However, he would need at least three or four rum and cokes before he would finally invade the dance floor.

It was during one of our earlier trips to Benidorm that we became friendly with a Flemish couple - Maria and Leo Dekkers - and they are still our dear friends to this day. They had been wintering in Benidorm for several years before we met them, and we got to know several of their very interesting friends as a result. One never-to-be-forgotten occasion was when we all went in four cars to a remote place high in the mountains beyond Aitana. The place had been originally a holiday building for nuns and was known as Le Couvent. It has since become a shelter for mountain goats! The purpose of our trip was to have a picnic, but also to bring back sacks of goat manure in the car boots for gardening purposes in Calpe. A close friend of Maria's, Juan, who managed a restaurant in Benidorm, took with him all the ingredients and pans to make a paella. He also took plenty of wine and a huge Spanish loaf as big as a washing-up bowl, and other necessities for a picnic. There, up in the mountains, on that sunny February noon, he made a fire and cooked the most wonderful paella I have ever tasted in my life. The fresh Spanish bread was torn off the huge loaf, and bread and paella were washed down with red wine from a giant-sized container.

THE APARTMENT

About fourteen years ago Mary and Jim decided to invest in a small holiday apartment. After a 'buy your own villa inspection flight to the Costa del Sol' which did not impress them, Mary went with me to Benidorm for a week to assess the apartment scene there. Jim could not be with us. We spent the week scouting round and chasing up ads in the *Costa Blanca News.* Near the end of the week we had narrowed the choice down to two possible apartments. One was on the twentieth floor of a magnificent apartment block, which got the sun all day in the winter; the other was a charming apartment which backed on to the mountains and therefore got less sun. We decided that Jim would much prefer the privacy of the twentieth floor. The couple who owned the mountain-facing apartment, Charlie and Ann Waddell, were so charming it was very difficult to tell them we had chosen '20E'. Nevertheless we later became great friends and we eventually found ourselves living in the same block. Charlie, like me, had a great love of all sport, and we are still close friends to this day.

With twenty-four hours to go, Mary and I had to settle the purchase. With the help of her credit card and also of mine, and the good services of Raoul, the president of the apartment block, the deposit was duly down and the deal clinched. Later, the contract was sealed and delivered under the auspices of Inga, the multi-lingual, tennis-playing factotum of the Notary's office. Inga became one of our friends and we enjoyed many a good game of tennis together. The apartment proved a real godsend to me - no more dissembling on package holidays! I could board a plane with my dog collar there for all to see, knowing that at Alicante Airport I would be slipping away to my own little world. There was the joy of being able to come and go as one pleased, with no worries about mealtimes . . . no long hours of talking shop in hotel lounges!

I had discovered a church called El Carmen on the Avenida Mediterranée. When I first went to Benidorm we had Mass there in a cellar which gradually grew to a first-floor church. Later, there was added an identical second-floor church. The whole project was the work of local boy made good, Padre Juan Serrano. The Serrano family had originally lived in Vilajoyosa and had owned most of the land between there and Benidorm. Originally Juan had the dream that he could build up an apartment block on this prime site, which would be a holiday and retirement complex for priests. However, the Cardinal in Madrid at the time did not have similar ideas and failed to support the scheme, and Padre Juan had to use his considerable business acumen and family resources to recoup his massive outlay. However, his 'double-decker church' proved to be, I'm sure, the most popular place of worship in the whole of Spain!

There were eleven Masses every weekend, thronged by ten thousand worshippers, and several of the Masses would actually double up - if by twenty-past six on Saturday or Sunday evening the lower church was already full, then the people would be directed up the marble steps to the upper church. By the start of Mass time at 6.30 p.m. both churches would be packed with 1,600 people. Then one of the priests would go upstairs, and take over a separate Mass there at the same time as the Mass was taking place in the lower church. Forty minutes later the scene would be reminiscent of a post-match scene at Roker Park when the crowds would be thronging the stairs leading out of the Roker End!

I became good friends with Padre Juan twenty years ago and he always appreciated my help. For many years now we have done a 'double act' at the 9.30 a.m. Latin Mass on Sundays. We would have the 'Readings' done both in Spanish and English, and he and I would provide a three-minute homily, first in Spanish and then in English. It was all very streamlined - the congregation would be out in forty minutes, making room for the crowds who were thronging the steps for the 10.30 Mass to follow!

For years I just used to 'attend' Mass and kneel in the benches. One day, however, a retired Dutch Jesuit missionary prevailed on me to come to the altar and concelebrate. I learnt the Second Eucharistic Prayer by heart in Spanish, and have been helping Padre Juan every day since then. Now of course, I have learnt sufficient Spanish to get by in any case. Many of my priest friends like to 'take a break' from saying Mass on holiday altogether . . . personally, I have always regarded my daily concelebration with Juan as a discipline, as well as a help to him for he could easily have three or four hundred communicants at most weekday Masses. I was delighted when I learned on my last visit that Juan had been made an episcopal vicar by his bishop in Alicante. At long last, Mother Church has recognized his wonderful work in one of the busiest parishes in the world.

One other little memory of Benidorm I must share with you. My ministry on one occasion was extended way beyond the portals of El Carmen. Margit Cohen, the Jewish lady who had sold the apartment to Mary, Jim and myself, had married again after the death of her husband. Her second husband, Reg, whom I knew well, had died suddenly while they were holidaying in South Africa. Poor Margit had brought his ashes home to Benidorm. Reg always had a great love for the rocky headland in Benidorm which divides the Levante beach and the Poniente beach. It is called La Cala. He had asked Margit that, in the event of his death, his ashes should be scattered in the sea near to the La Cala, rocky sea wall. Margit did not know any Rabbi in Benidorm, but I had often stood in informally for the rabbi in my early priestly days in Sunderland, and I had frequently been involved in counselling sessions with the young Jewish community there. Margit thought that as a minister, and a friend, I could deputize for the absent Rabbi. I donned my priestly all-purpose alb and stole, and we had a twenty-minute farewell service with Christian hymns and prayers down at La Cala. By the time we finished we had gathered quite a crowd of curious passers-by who no doubt wondered what it was all about. Margit duly emptied the urn into the sea swell of La Cala on a glorious sunny afternoon. Afterwards, we all returned to her large apartment for refreshments. Margit is an extremely talented painter and she insisted on my choosing one of her very special paintings as my 'stipend'! A beautiful Benidorm sunset with 'M. Cohen' inscribed in the bottom right-hand corner adorns the wall of our apartment to this day.

In recent years Benidorm has become quite a superior resort. Millions of pesetas have been spent on it by the local council and the Spanish Tourist Board. The two beaches, with their beautiful promenades which stretch for five miles, have been pedestrianized. Every night, every inch of the golden sand is cleaned and smoothed over. The Aiguera Park has been constructed and houses two beautiful open-air, Grecian-style amphitheatres. The local *Policia* have clamped down very heavily on the 'lager louts' and removed all trace of drunkenness and rowdy behaviour. Misbehaviour of this kind can result in immediate imprisonment and deportation on the next plane home. A magnificent sports complex has also been built next to the Benidorm football ground, where I frequently enjoy tennis games with friends who have been holidaying with me.

There are of course some Spanish tennis partners who I have known for years, like Valencian dentist Luis Linares and his friend Garbi, who has herself become a regular tennis partner for me in the last five or six years.

One of the great joys of holidaying in an apartment for me has been the opportunity to cook in a leisurely manner. I find it wonderfully relaxing. I once took Arthur Kelly, God rest him, to Benidorm. He assured my parishioners in Sedgefield on our return that 'Father Caden only has one meal a day in Benidorm . . . but it lasts all day!' I must say, I never found Arthur refusing any dish I set before him. I love to get out my wok, and prepare a leisurely Coq au Vin inspired by a martini bianco on the rocks, one of my favourite drinks. I have an old video player out there too, so I usually accompany all this with a couple of episodes of Rigsby in *Rising Damp.* I have probably seen them dozens of times, but I still find Leonard Rossiter one of the funniest men who ever lived. He provides some wonderful company for me while the wok is simmering.

Mary and Jim no longer go to the apartment as regularly as they did. However, Vera loves to go and take her friends Monica or Theresa with her, or various members of her family. Over the years, she has decorated and improved the apartment, occasionally with a little help from her brother Gerard. She has improved the furnishings so much that it is now like a small Spanish home. Her niece Veronica and Veronica's husband, Robert, and their children, Marie and Darren, love to go with her. The children especially have adored the place as they were growing up. I am always delighted when they decide to go . . . I hope that they will always continue to enjoy Apartment 20!

CHAPTER XXX

EDUCATION - CONNECTIONS

My escapes to Benidorm were always opportunities for me to recharge my batteries. Having retired from the County Council in 1989 and having my links with the Health Authority severed in 1990, I did not have time to get any withdrawal symptoms. More work, especially in the field of education, came my way. I continued as a member of the County Education Committee, but now representing the diocese instead of the people of Sedgefield. There are fifty or so Catholic Schools in Durham County, and so it is quite a large responsibility. This responsibility also means automatic membership of the Diocesan Schools Commission and other sub-committees. My chairmanship of Carmel School Governing Body naturally continues to make increasing demands on my time.

The school has become very popular and numbers have increased rapidly. The appointment of a new headmaster in 1993 - Mr Jim O'Neill - and a new deputy head, Maura Regan, gave the school a very sound disciplinary and pastoral base. Hundreds of parents, in-cluding many non-Catholic parents, showed their approval by besieging the school to gain admission for their children. Jim O'Neill is a workaholic and he also demands one hundred per cent commitment from his staff. A lot of hard work, and a little good luck gained for us Technology College status. This allowed us to attract some bright, young, highly qualified and dedicated staff to cope with the ever increasing pupil numbers. Jim used his management team of Maura, Julie Jasper, Colm Doyle and Mike Rudd to great advantage. They were backed up by some excellent heads of department, and a very high tone prevails throughout the school. At the same time I continued to enjoy my chairmanship of our joint primary school at Trimdon St Williams. Pat McTimoney had succeeded my first head, John Hannon, and has been doing a great job there. Sadly she is now working her early retirement.

Nevertheless, we are inevitably fast running out of priests as Chairmen of Governors and Education Authority members. With the Darlington Unitary Authority Education Committee now established I have agreed to represent the diocese on it for the present, as well as continuing to be a member of the Durham County Education Authority. Perhaps in the near future there will emerge some lay experts in the field of education who will be happy to take over the roles formerly held only by priests in the diocese. Ministry to Priests, I am pleased to write, is still continuing to give us great support. Our theatre group continues to flourish with the help of the extra overnight venue of Ushaw College. The Council of Priests and its ad hoc working parties are still involving me with extra satisfying work. Bishop Ambrose, when he arrived in the diocese, opted to appoint me as 'Chairman' of his Council of Priests from the start. I think that this, in practice, is a better way for an elected council to do business. Ambrose presides at all the meetings, but it is easy to know exactly when he wants to make an intervention. A priest chairman, with the bishop as president, seems to have worked very well. It also enables the bishop to use his chairman to organize working parties and subcommittees at various levels.

ALDERMAN

When I retired from the elected membership of the County Council in 1989, I was quite delighted to be given the honour of becoming an Honorary Alderman of the County. Councillor Jim Graham, a lovely man and Chairman of the Council at the time, conferred the honour on me. I was probably in a unique position to enjoy it. Unlike other aldermen, I had not severed my working links with the County Council. I was still going into County Hall maybe four or five times a month to represent the diocese on the Education Committee and the Youth and Community Committee, and am still doing so as I write these memoirs.

The past Chairman of the County Council, Councillor Joe Walker, had a special place for the aldermen. He not only wined and dined them at Christmas time, but insisted on inviting them to be his guests at the Riverside County Cricket Ground on two occasions. Joe did a great job in his two years as chairman, despite struggling with health handicaps, and a hip replacement operation. He succeeded, by his fairness, in making all members of the County Council feel that they had a valuable part to play. Many years ago he had worked hard with me in running that very successful football team in St Patrick's, Dipton. His last act of kindness to me as Chairman of Durham County Council was to invite me and a party of my own choosing to be his guests yet once more at the Riverside. He carefully concealed from me, until I arrived there, that the guests *he* had chosen on that day were to be Phil McNulty, Des Bell and Mattie Gowland - three of the key men of the Pat's team of thirty-five years before. It was one of the most wonderful surprises of my life! Even though the rain prevented any cricket that day, we nevertheless had a wonderful reunion. Thank you, Joe!

THE PENSIONERS' PARLIAMENT

In 1993 the European Parliament decided to organize a week in Luxembourg, when an elected pensioner from every one of the 518 constituencies in the EEC would form a Pensioners' Parliament for a working week, using the exact debating mode of the European Parliament itself. I was elected from a short list of twelve to represent Stephen Hughes's constituency of Durham and Blaydon. Stephen gave me tremendous support. Indeed, many of my fellow pensioner-parliamentarians envied me, that I had such a supportive and excellent MEP in Durham.

It became obvious to me during that week that Stephen was very highly regarded by his colleagues in Europe. I think I was chosen because of my long experience in local government and in the NHS, and also in parish life. I was articulate enough to be able to move quite comfortably in the debating company of some of the very high profile performers in Europe. The level of debate - instantly translated

Caricature - the Author at the EEC Pensioners' Parliament, Luxembourg

into nine languages for all the five hundred plus members - was very high. Certainly it made House of Commons standards look quite pale! I was privileged to make a two-and-a-half-minute speech about the Social Chapter and the NHS, and was able to point out as a priest how certain passages from the Social Chapter legislation were 'word for word' translations of the two Papal Encyclicals of 1891 and 1931 - '*Rerum Novarum*' and '*Quadragesimo Anno*'. Timing was of the essence: at the end of one's two and a half minutes, the chairperson simply switched off the speaking member's microphone, and consequently the remainder of ones words were lost as far as the debate was concerned - ruthless but effective!

I had the privilege of working closely with ex-Trade Union boss, Jack Jones. How the years have mellowed Jack, and made him a much more effective politician. In addition to Stephen Hughes's prompting and guidance, we were well 'chaperoned' by a dynamic lady called Pauline Green - a London MEP who has since become leader of the whole Socialist group in the European Parliament. When I returned to England I was drafted in by my friend Cindy Hughes, Stephen's wife, to address a number of pensioners' rallies throughout the North-East. I suspect that the charming Cindy may have thought that I was a trifle radical for a non-politician, but one cannot spend nearly fifty years working with the sick and the marginalized in society without their needs becoming part of one's own life.

CHAPTER XXXI

SUNDERLAND EMPIRE REVISITED

As you will recall from some earlier pages, the Sunderland Empire held some wonderful memories for me as a young priest. It had been the focus of my Catholic Stage Guild Apostolate, which had resulted from the direct intervention of the Cardinal and Wee Georgie Wood. It had been the one and only time when Westminster had taken any part in shaping my priesthood. Even though at that time I was not 'allowed' to enjoy a show from the auditorium, my work backstage produced many very satisfying spiritual results, and made me many friends.

In my early days I suppose I had a great love of the theatre, which of necessity had to be a frustrated one. I had really enjoyed my appearances on the college stage at Ushaw beginning with a single line debut shouting 'tomatoes' at crucial moments in the comedy on offer. Eventually I aspired to a possibly over-acted 'witch' in Macbeth. I say over-acted advisedly because in the middle of one of the live performances the imitation fire under our cauldron actually began to burn and I was trying to extinguish the potential flames with my bare hands with witch-like shrieks to make it seem all like part of the show. Later on I had my biggest part, the part of Wargrave, the crazy judge-murderer in what at that time was then known as the thriller - *Ten Little Niggers* . . . That was of course in the days prior to political correctness! I remember as a youngster at Ushaw when Gilbert and Sullivan was all the rage, and I thrilled to the masterly Mikado of Father Tom Morton, later a Shrewsbury Diocesan priest. Tom was a big man with a fine voice and a wonderful stage presence. He was made to look even taller by the black plumes rising from his head-dress. For years playing the Mikado himself was one of my personal fantasies! However, by the time I was myself appearing on the college stage, musicals had disappeared in favour of straight plays. Once I was officially allowed to enjoy theatre after 1965 I saw many a Mikado. Finally, I saw Tom Morton's interpretation matched by a D'Oyle Carte version where the Mikado was 'built up' to be huge, and commanding the whole stage.

My nearest approach to taking part in a musical at Ushaw was as a producer. A Middlesbrough diocesan priest named after the martyr Oliver Plunkett had himself written a very funny musical. 'Olly' was a natural as a funny man, whether delivering his own parodies with banjo immortalizing some of our more notorious Ushaw professors at that time, or bringing down the house with some comedy vignettes in *The Amazing Dr Clitterhouse.* He was a big man with one of the most expressive faces you ever saw. In later years the good people of Bridlington would find Olly's preaching a wonderful asset to their worship. Certainly he had served his apprenticeship well at Ushaw. In the musical he wrote he had used everything from grand opera down to pop to provide the musical vehicle for his own very funny lyrics. He had been warned by the authorities of the college that he must concentrate more on Theology and less on the Thespian Art. Consequently, his final masterpiece had to be fairly cautious . . . using me as a front. Although I was on the credits as the producer, everyone knew that the 'real maestro' behind the whole production was Olly. It was wonderful to see him again recently at the Golden Jubilee Mass of our mutual friend Canon Louis Collingwood!

But where was I when I began my theatrical nostalgia trip? Oh yes, back at the Sunderland Empire on 21 November 1996. A group of priests had been raising money for charity for several years with a show called *The Clergy Review* (named after a well-known priestly monthly magazine). The year 1996 was the fortieth year of publication for our diocesan newspaper, *Northern Cross.* To celebrate this, it was decided that the Hexham and Newcastle priests would do their own *Clergy Review* at the Sunderland Empire. Thinking that it would attract the full support of all the priestly talent in the diocese, I agreed to take part. Unfortunately, there was only a limited response, priestwise! The review had to be bolstered up by several very professional acts from the people of God. Possibly this was fortuitous, because the eventual review was a brilliant two and a half hours of wonderful entertainment.

The comedy of Father Wilf McConnell and Father Mick McKenna was already legendary, and they compered the whole show between them with a professionalism that kept the sell-out crowd roaring with laughter every time they appeared on stage. The only other priests in sight were Father Tony Cornforth with an 'abbreviated' folksong duet - there were really too many acts finally on offer and pruning was the order of the evening - and the Chancey Brothers, of course, were the Cass brothers, Tom and Dick supported by Father Pat O'Connell.

Rounding off the priestly acts was an offering from Father Dick Harriott and 'yours truly'. I went on stage to sing Paul Robeson's 'Shorten'n Bread' - certainly the most hackneyed song in the Caden repertoire. It was always in demand from the nuns at Oak Lea and Somerleyton Convents . . . probably several grandparents in the Empire that night must have heard it forty years before when they were part of St Mary's School or St Mary's Club. Indeed, the first person I actually spotted on leaving the stage door was one of my old Youth Club boys with his grandchildren! When Dick and I finally majestically strolled on stage with our policemens' helmets and very realistic truncheons - fashioned by our versatile site manager/lab technician at Carmel School, Frank Ryder - we certainly looked the part. Offenbach's 'Gendarmes Duet' is a guaranteed 'show stopper' even with a couple of very average bass-baritones . . . and that night was no exception. With a polished accompaniment from Carmel's music genius, Andrew Ramsey, and his charming assistant Claire Appleton, we really enjoyed ourselves!

My mind went back forty-two years. I remembered the Val Doonican of the Four Ramblers Days coming off stage at the Empire with an animated smile as the applause died away . . . With tremendous enthusiasm he would be telling me 'we really tore them up tonight Father!' Forty-four years before, when I began my Catholic Stage Guild apostolate, I never dreamt for a moment that there would come a day when I would help entertain a capacity crowd at the Sunderland Empire itself!

CHAPTER XXXII

LABOUR GETS A NEW LEADER

It was on 12 May 1994 that the nation reeled at the stunning news that John Smith, the Leader of the Opposition, had died suddenly from a heart attack. The Shadow Home Secretary, Tony Blair, and the Shadow Chancellor, Gordon Brown, were the front-runners in the impending leadership election. They were the modernisers in the party and many saw them as most likely to continue the work of Neil Kinnock and of John Smith, who had just died so prematurely and tragically.

Tony and Gordon were good friends and they quickly agreed that they would not split the moderniser vote. It must have taken great strength of character and realism on Gordon Brown's part, nevertheless, Tony quickly emerged as the main contender for the leadership and was duly elected by a huge majority. At the time I became something of a media personality in responding to repeated demands from TV, radio and newspapers to throw some light on Blair the man, Blair the tennis player, Blair the family man and Blair the Christian. In the run-up to the leadership contest, John Burton, Tony's agent, and one of his closest friends politically as well as on the level of pure friendship, was naturally besieged by the media. John knew me well - we had been close friends since 1973. I had also been a governor of Sedgefield Community College where John had been head of PE, until his early retirement through an arthritic condition. After his own interviews with the media, they would usually ask John who they could interview in the community. Since I have never been a member of a political party, and was a well-known personality, both in the local authority and NHS fields, I was a natural. With John's directions they would find their way unerringly down to St John Fisher, Sedgefield and get to work on me. Quite naturally, I felt that anything I could say which would make my friend more electable as leader of his party was completely worthwhile, even though it might frequently take several hours work to achieve it. This sometimes meant that I would be spending a couple of hours donning vestments in my church and answering all kinds of questions about my friendship with Tony, what kind of man he was and how his gospel values influenced his political life. Eventually, after all this, a twenty-second sound bite would appear on *Newsnight* or some similar TV programme. The same process, only multiplied many times more, was repeated in the 1997 Election Campaign. This time, however, it was the *world's media* rather than just the *British media.*

THE ELECTION

John Major decided to call a 1 May election on 17 March. It might have been that he thought an imminent report on the controversial 'Cash for Questions Issue' would further damage his party's electoral chances if properly debated in the House of Commons. Alternatively, it might have been that he personally thought that, with the opinion polls indicating that the Tories were 20 per cent behind New Labour, he needed six weeks to convince the electorate rather than the usual four. What we do know now, with hindsight, is that the whole strategy went completely wrong. There resulted the most devastating landslide defeat for a government that I can remember. Devastating, especially in the loss of so many ministerial figures and the wiping out of any Conservative presence at all in Scotland and Wales. An overall majority for Tony Blair's New Labour of 177 seats with 44.4 per cent share of the vote was a result, only to be *dreamt* rather than actually *achieved*! Tony Blair had not only by his courageous leadership transformed New Labour into an electable party, but had actually obtained the strongest mandate for his comparatively moderate policies, by Labour standards, ever given to a Prime Minister in my lifetime.

By an unexpected quirk of fate a septugenarian priest became an integral part of an extraordinary series of events which ended in Downing Street. I was whisked away from Teesside Airport in a private Suckling Airways, sixty-seater prop jet, headed for Stansted Airport.

The champagne corks were popping during the 45-minute flight. In no time we were speeding from Stansted to the Festival Hall for the official 5 a.m. party.

As we were leaving the bus, a TV interview was concluding with one of the former Shadow Cabinet - he humbly commented on 'the awesome responsibility implicit in the sheer size of such a mandate'. These sentiments later would be emphasized by the new Prime Minister when he addressed his 417 MPs in Westminster Hall before the work of government began. His words would be a reminder to all of them, and indeed to us in our lives: 'Remember always that we are the servants and not the masters.'

The Festival Hall was undergoing large-scale repair work. Our conveyance, a Labout Election bus, had no difficulty in gaining entrance, which is more than can be said for the Prime Minister's car. John Burton and Jonathan Powell were in the accompanying car leading the way from Stansted to the Festival Hall. John had to circle the Hall twice before he was able to gain an entrance. Eventually he and Jonathan Powell had to convince the police that they were trying to find an entrance for the Prime Minister. We were already in the Hall when John finally got the Prime Minister inside.

I was a little taken aback with the galaxy of talent, both theatrical and political: Richard Branson, with entourage, flanked by Richard Attenborough, Tony Booth, Sinead Cusack and many others I did not see immediately. Then there was a host of political figures, including Neil Kinnock, Peter Mandleson, Gordon Brown and John Prescott, to name but a few.

As a political observer, I think that the 'time for change factor' was so much stronger after eighteen years, than it had been when Neil Kinnock led the party in 1992. This factor of course had been strengthened by an appalling record of 'sleaze', both moral and financial. Even ministers, let alone back-benchers, never felt it their duty to resign or even to say '*Mea Culpa*'. Many of the earlier reforms of the Tory Party, especially in the 1980s, had been sound, but afterwards they embraced continuing reform and privatization as an ideology to be pushed through for its own sake. Furthermore, John Major, himself a decent and very likeable man, allowed himself to be pushed by a rump of Europhobes into tolerating growing xenophobia in his party, which was to destroy any semblence of unity on the whole question of Europe. The party that had taken us into Europe was now giving such discordant, conflicting signals to the electorate that the hope of real courageous leadership was perceived to be in the Blair factor rather than in the Major record. At a purely local level an interesting development is possibly worthy of comment. Fifteen months before the Election on a very snowy day I had a charming young visitor to the Presbytery. My caller was Liz Noel, the daughter of the well-known Catholic writer Gerard Noel. She told me that she was to be the Conservative candidate in our Sedgefield constituency. She was carrying out her father's instructions by introducing herself to the priest!

Now I have alwats encouranged our committed Catholics to take an active part in public life, especially at local authority level, in whatever party they are espoused. I gave Liz a very warm welcome and promised her my continuing friendship. She knew of course that I was a friend of the Blairs, and also that Tony had worshipped in my church scores of times since 1983. Later, I described her very truthfully in the *Catholic Herald* as a 'breath of fresh air in Conservative politics'. By the time her political ambition was to face the ultimate test as one of Tony's opponents last May, she had married Henry Pitman. I hope that she will persevere in the political field - maybe next time in some more winnable seat! At least next time, Liz, you may not have the albatross of Europe hanging about your winsome neck!

The excitement of those final days was unbelievable. In the six weeks leading up to 1 May, John Burton, Tony's agent had dispatched in my direction Dutch TV, German TV, Sky TV, GMTV and BBC TV, as well as Australian, Belgian and Canadian Radio; and several correspondents including *Time Magazine* and European correspondents. I must have given twenty hours of interviews! But, increasingly, I sensed with confidence that my tiny contribution was to the inevitable victory of a man whose whole life was based on the *conviction* of his gospel values, rather than on the occasional *lip-service* paid to them by so many politicians.

It was the insistence of GMTV Breakfast television to have me with John Burton 'live' in their London Studios on the Friday morning after the election, which led to my sharing in the incredible triumph of Downing Street on Friday, 2 May 1997, as described in the short

John Burton and the Author before their breakfast television interview on GMTV the morning after the Election

opening chapter of this book! Catherine Maloftsky of GMTV tenaciously pursued me by phone in the last five days preceding 2 May. She would 'fly me' down to London the night before, and book me into a nearby hotel - Catherine is a very persuasive lady, although sadly I never met her when I got to the studios, or when, ten days later, I was invited to be interviewed at length on the Sunday morning *A Matter of Faith*. However, Tony's Press Secretary, Anna Healey, talked to her, and when convinced that a Tyne-Tees studio interview would not do, told Catherine that I would be given a lift on one of the chartered planes that would be leaving Teesside Airport for Stanstead about 3 a.m. in the morning on the Friday. No doubt Anna was worried about the excitement and strain of being up all night on a 73-year-old. And so I became part of the Festival Hall celebration and later the Downing Street triumph. Thank you, Catherine, for your persistence! Thank you, Anna, for your thoughtfulness!

CHAPTER XXXIII

NEARLY FIFTY YEARS . . . BUT WHEN I LOOK BACK

On 25 July 1998 I will give thanks to God for fifty years in His service as well as thirteen years spent preparing for that service; that is, if He spares me until that very special day. You will see from the preceding pages that so much has happened in that period that I have only been able to hint at some of the ecclesiastical trends and of their impact. Without doubt, 'churchwise', the Vatican Council of the early 1960s was the most momentous event of the century. It altered the whole stance of the Catholic Church. After it, we were no longer an island surrounded by dangerous waters and currents, loath to concede even a fraction of our coastline to these elements.

Suddenly we perceived our huge, numerical Catholic strength of eight or nine hundred millions as a powerful base for integration with the billions outside us, rather than a base for proud isolation. The indefatigable journeys of John Paul II, his speeches, encyclicals and his desire to embrace the troubles and hopes of billions of people all over the world, had a huge impact on the way Catholics were now perceived in the world. The 'Church' now meant something completely different for me in the 1990s, compared with my idea of it in the 1950s. Inevitably, the concept of being a Christian, rather than a Catholic, had huge implications for anyone under fifty. Millions of our younger people had never known the 'Old Church' at all; they had never seen a 'penny' catechism. Inevitably, in the West, our church attendances gradually showed up to a 20 per cent decline as people saw their relationship with God in a completely different way. As noted earlier, the God of Fear had given way to the God of Love! And yet in the Third World and the emerging nations the story was completely the opposite - vocations to the priesthood were flourishing there and increasing. The frightening decline of vocations in the West was offset by a huge rise in the number of priests being ordained in the Third World.

This dearth of vocations in the West, however, has numerous implications for us. I have observed that the more affluent a people is, then the less likely are its youth to be prepared to make the sacrifices necessary for priesthood. As a post-Vatican II Church, we have rightly put the 'Eucharist' at the forefront of our agenda. In the last decade, we have worked hard to produce a collaborative ministry with our lay people, which is precisely what Christ intended from the beginning. Nevertheless, even though we are still just managing to cope in the provision of the Eucharist in the West, in five years' time, given the present decline in vocations, we will of necessity be struggling to provide even a weekly Mass in many areas, let alone a daily one.

One of the most obvious ways to alleviate the problem is to accept the possibility of a voluntary celibacy in the priesthood, even though it won't cure it. In recent years we have been glad to ordain hundreds of former Anglican and Episcopalian priests, many of whom are married. They have fitted in very well into the pastoral scene, this despite previous worries that our older generation would never accept such a development. Many of this older generation were geared to weekly, if not daily Mass. They are pragmatic enough to want the Eucharist, whatever changes may be necessary to continue providing it. They have been delighted to accept lay Eucharistic ministers, especially when they themselves have become less mobile or even housebound in their declining years. The Church needs sufficient vision and courage to grasp the nettle.

Maybe, too, there are a number of priests who left the priesthood because they found the burden of celibacy too much, who would be only too delighted to be employed in their priestly ministry once more. What a wonderful, Christ-like gesture it would be to mark the Millennium, if bishops throughout the world were empowered to offer an amnesty to all those priests who had left the active ministry, because they discovered too late they did not have a vocation to celibacy. We older priests are humbly only too well aware of the outstanding qualities of so many of our former colleagues who were compelled to disappear from the clerical scene A two-stream priesthood with a celibate priesthood working harmoniously and efficaciously alongside a married priesthood, could be something well worth trying. We owe it to the vast majority of our Eucharistic communities. The Eucharist is the centre of our Catholic life; if people are deprived of it then we miss the whole reason for our ministry. Maybe it is now time for us finally and humbly to admit that a vocation to priesthood is not necessarily a vocation to celibacy. Let's clear the way before it is too late!

In my early priesthood celibacy still had a prophetic value. In my extensive youth apostolate of the 1950s in Sunderland, I was vividly aware that my celibacy did have such a value . . . yes, and among non-churched young people as well! This awareness, coupled with an often exhausting fourteen-hour day, made celibacy just attainable for me. Forty years on, however, I am convinced it no longer has that same prophetic value, even for our Catholic youth, let alone for those outside our portals. Through my work as Chairman of the Carmel School Governing Body I am still in almost daily contact with the Church of tomorrow - our teenagers. I am convinced that not only do they perceive celibacy as an outdated notion, but most of them have little if any idea of what priesthood is really about. In the 1950s there were hundreds of young priests around in our diocese and other dioceses who could be role models for our youngsters. For some years in Darlington, Father Dave Russell has been the only young priest on the pastoral scene! He has done a wonderful job as Chaplain to Carmel School as well as in the Darlington community. Fifty years ago young Catholics were knee-deep in role models - nowadays, it would take an extensive search to uncover even the isolated ones. No wonder that for thousands of our youngsters Channel 4's award winning *Father Ted* is their only insight into *priesthood.* The caricature has become the reality for many! Sadly, priesthood has also been grossly damaged in the last decade by a spate of scandals which I think have been reflected in our declining congregations. One of the very reasons, as stated in the Foreword, why I attempted these memoirs, was to debunk the image of Father Ted. At least Father Clifford of *Ballykissangel* - the most recent of our TV priestly soaps - is slightly more in tune with the priesthood of the 1950s! The rumour, though, is that he too is destined for laicization.

Recently, a friend asked me if I had any regrets as I approached my '50th'. I had to think hard for some time. You see, I have enjoyed my priesthood immensely, and all its extra dimensions. Maybe the extra dimensions kept it fresh for me. Certainly, I can honestly say at seventy-four I still get a 'buzz' at the thought of sharing the Gospel Message three times every weekend with my long-suffering flock. Perhaps my flock don't always get the same buzz, but then when you have been talking to the same 130 families for thirty-one years it is not easy to keep it fresh all the time.

If I had to be ruthlessly honest, I would have to admit that, unlike the claims of some leaders of my Church, my celibacy was rarely a joy after the first fifteen years of priesthood. It was always a very hard struggle . . . a struggle which, as I got older, I sometimes only survived by the narrowest of margins!

Maybe I was lucky that nearly all my priesthood was spent in parishes where I was working all the hours that God sent so I never had time to allow myself to lick my wounds or to brood. In any case, my priesthood made for me many warm and supportive friendships which ensured that I was generally 'happy in my work'. If there had to be a regret at all, it is in the knowledge, as I canter into the third age, 'that I never had the joy of my own children, let alone the joy of grandchildren'. But you might quite rightly retort: 'Game, set and match means you win some, but you don't necessarily win them all!'